The Nuts & Bolts of Active Learning

Purposeful, Successful Strategies for Every Classroom

By The Nuts & Bolts Family of Educators

Kim Campbell

Sharon Faber

Cherrie Farnette

Marjorie Frank

Jodie Fransen

Kathy Hunt-Ullock

Mark McLeod

Jill Norris

Melba Richardson

Dave Sanders

Monte Selby

Debbie Silver

Dedra Stafford

Randy Thompson

Rick Wormeli

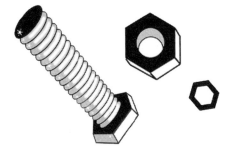

The proceeds of this book support, in part, a scholarship for educators to attend the Nuts & Bolts Symposiums.

Illustrated by Kathleen Bullock
Edited by Marjorie Frank and Jill Norris
Copyedited by Cary Grayson

ISBN 978-0-86530-693-6

2   3   4   5   6   7   8   9   10   12   11   10

Printed by Sheridan Books, Inc., Chelsea, Michigan • September 2010
www.incentivepublications.com

Getting Down to the Nuts and Bolts

When you get down to the nuts and bolts of any subject you take a close look at the basic facts. In *The Nuts & Bolts of Active Learning*, the family of amazing, award-winning educators who collaborate with attendees at the annual Nuts & Bolts Symposiums held in Destin, Boulder, Dallas, and Nashville share their favorite active learning strategies. These 20 experts get down to the basics with strategies that will engage your students in active learning.

Active learning involves providing opportunities for students to meaningfully talk and listen, write, read, and reflect on the content, ideas, issues, and concerns of an academic subject.

Meyers & Jones, 1993

In fact, sitting for more than ten minutes at a stretch "reduces our awareness of physical and emotional sensations and increases fatigue." This results in reduced concentration and, most likely, discipline problems.

Eric Jenson

Students are not passive receptors into which teachers deposit concepts and information.

Active learning is a multi-directional learning experience in which learning occurs teacher-to-student, student-to-teacher, and student-to-student.

Mel Silberman

For middle school boys whose bodies are experiencing between five and seven spikes per day of the aggression hormone, testosterone, physical movement is crucial.

Michael Gurian

When a human sits for longer than about 17 minutes, blood begins to pool in the hamstrings and calf muscles pulling needed oxygen and glucose from the brain. Melatonin kicks in because the brain thinks it's at rest. The learner gets lethargic and sleepy and struggles to focus. Learning declines. Movement is the body's way of balancing itself physically, chemically, electrically, and emotionally.

What Is Active Learning?

Active learning

- engages students cognitively and physically in the learning process
- provides students opportunities to manipulate, apply, evaluate, and generally interact with concepts
- encourages students to generate information rather than simply receive it
- requires students to reflect on what they are doing—connecting course concepts with their experiences, generating and asking meaningful questions, searching for answers, interacting with new reading material
- forces students to think about and comment on new learning

What Does Active Learning Look Like?

Students are involved. They

- act, move, think, write, discuss, read, and investigate
- solve problems
- ask questions
- respond to ideas
- engage in higher-order thinking tasks—analyzing, synthesizing, and evaluating information.
- collaborate and cooperate with others
- explore their attitudes and values
- self-reflect on ideas
- reflect on ideas in discussion with others

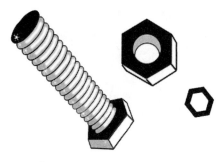

What Are the Benefits of Active Learning?

Research on active learning and brain-compatible learning shows us that students who actively engage with material

- learn more
- are more likely to remember what they learn
- retain information longer
- attend to lessons better
- enjoy classes more
- have higher levels of motivation
- have better attitudes toward learning
- connect material to their real lives
- develop a deeper understanding of material
- demonstrate better thinking and writing skills
- take responsibility for their own learning
- become lifelong learners

In addition, active learning strategies serve students with a variety of learning styles, and offer teachers great flexibility to differentiate instruction and assessment.

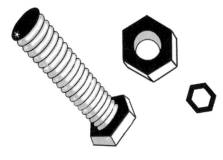

Table of Contents

Strategy #1

Creative Nuts and Bolts

Real nuts and bolts are used to learn about the nuts and bolts of creative thinking.

What to Use

- several dozen nuts and bolts of varying sizes
- containers for nuts and bolts (one for each group)
- pencils and large sheets of paper (for each group)
- clock or timer

What to Do

1. Divide students into groups of four. Give each group a container of nuts and bolts along with paper and pencils.

2. Introduce students to these facets of creative thinking: fluency (the ability to come up with lots of different ideas), flexibility (the ability to come up with different kinds of ideas), and originality (the ability to come up with ideas that are out of the ordinary).

3. Tell students that you will set a timer for three minutes. In that time, they will brainstorm uses for nuts and bolts (singly, together, or in a group). Encourage them to try for lots of ideas, but also to think "outside the box" for different categories and original ideas.

4. Set the timer for four minutes. Stop the brainstorming.

5. Have each group join another group and share the lists quickly, crossing out any ideas that they have in common.

6. Give groups another two minutes to continue trying to expand the number, type, and originality of the ideas.

7. Take time to share all the lists. Groups should continue to cross out ideas that show up on other lists.

8. At the end, count all the many ideas. Note each group's original ideas—those that no other group had. Try some of them!

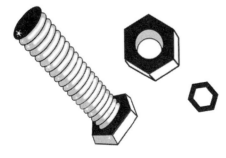

The Nuts & Bolts of Active Learning

 Strategy #2

Acts Of Caring

Students acknowledge other students for caring by creating and giving recognition cards.

What to Use

- paper, pencils, pens, and markers
- cards like the format below

What to Do

- Reproduce the recognition cards and have them available.
- Pairs of students award classmates for their acts of caring.

Acts of....

Being thoughtful

Kindness

unselfishness

FRIENDSHIP

SHARING

An Act of_____

Who? _____

What happened? _____

When? _____

Where? _____

Giving your time, energy, help, comfort, praise, and encouragement is often more important than giving things.

Strategy #3

Adhesive Note Graphs

Students move around the room and place answers to questions on bar graph templates using small adhesive notes. This activity allows students to see the answer in a colorful bar graph format.

What to Use

- a few LARGE pieces of bulletin board paper
- a dark marker
- a large number of adhesive notes in assorted colors

What to Do

1. Place a number of LARGE bar graphs around the room with the "x" axis labeled with possible multiple choice answers to a specific question, one question per graph.

2. Give each student a number of different-colored adhesive notes.

3. Label each possible answer on the "x" axis of each graph with a certain color adhesive note.

4. Have the students answer each of the questions on the graphs at their seats. Once this is completed, have the students take their papers and adhesive notes, walk around the room, look at each bar graph, choose the correct answer, match the color of the correct answer to a small adhesive note, write their names on the notes, and put the note on the graph.

5. Once the entire class has placed their notes on all of the graphs, one can readily see how the students responded to all questions.

6. Call out random students' names from the graph and ask them to explain why they responded as they did.

7. Finally, reveal the correct answer to each question.

Strategy #4

Be An Expert

Students become a character or take on a specific role to explore the text or concept from different viewpoints and to consider the results and implications of a specific action.

What to Use

- background information for student experts

What to Do

1. Identify the curricular topic or text to explore.
2. Brainstorm with class experts who could deal with the issue, what they would know, and what actions they might take.
3. Introduce a situation: the purpose of the activity, the roles to be played, and the audience, Together think about who would benefit from the knowledge offered by the experts.
5. Students choose specific roles, prepare, and plan.
6. Students assume their roles and are interviewed. The interviews may take the form of radio or television interviews or panels.

Explain how your viewpoint differs from some others.

Strategy #5

Braindump March

Students march around the room to high-energy, fast-paced music. When the music stops, students find partners and "empty" their brains.

What to Use

- music
- space for marching

What to Do

1. Following a mini lecture, play high-energy, fast-paced music.
2. Have students march. (You may need them to march in place if you do not have room for whole class movement.)
3. Stop the music. Students stop marching.
4. Students find partners and designate one person of the pair as #1 and one as #2.
5. On the signal, for 60 seconds, #1 tells everything he or she remembers about the topic of the mini lecture. Student #2's job is to listen actively.
6. Signal the end of 60 seconds; #2 continues without repeating anything #1 said. Student #1 listens.
7. At the end of the two minutes, turn the music back on and have students march back to their seats.

Gettyburg Battle was fought from July 1 to 3, 1863, in Gettysburg, Pennsylvania. It was considered the turning point in the Civil War. Union General George Gordon Meade and the Army of the Potomac fought General Robert E. Lee and the Confederates. General Lee hoped to invade Pennsylvania and trap the Union army in a vulnerable location. Lee crossed the Blue Ridge Mountains and Maryland and gathered his whole army at Gettysburg . . .

Time! Number Two, please tell us what you remember about the Battle of Gettysburg.

Strategy #6

"Can You Guess This?" Review

Students use their logical/analytical sense to create a unique kind of review. Teams generate factual statements about the topic of study for others to solve. Each statement must combine numbers and words in an equation that accurately reflects the subject material. This review is unique and quite fun for most students.

> P.E.
> **600 = N O O**
> **in a B I***
>
> *600 = Number of Outs in a Baseball Inning

What to Use

- chart paper and markers, or
- overhead transparency sheets and pens, or
- paper, pen, and document camera, or
- board and chalk or marker

What to Do

1. Students work in small teams to try and "stump" their peers by creating review facts written as equations:

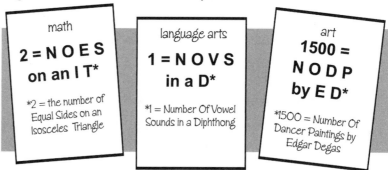

> math
> **2 = N O E S**
> **on an I T***
>
> *2 = the number of Equal Sides on an Isosceles Triangle

> language arts
> **1 = N O V S**
> **in a D***
>
> *1 = Number Of Vowel Sounds in a Diphthong

> art
> **1500 = N O D P by E D***
>
> *1500 = Number Of Dancer Paintings by Edgar Degas

2. Each team creates as many "equations" about the selected topic as possible and writes them on chart paper, a transparency sheet, or on paper.

3. Representatives for each team take turns presenting one of their team's "equations." No duplications are allowed.

4. The challenged teams have one minute to try and guess the equation. One responder from each team will raise his or her hand when they have a solution. The presenting representative calls on the representatives in the order their hands were raised. The first team to guess the correct answer scores a point. If no one guesses the answer within one minute (or a predetermined time), the presenting team receives one point (as long as the equation was written correctly about accurate subject matter).

5. Play continues until teams exhaust their equations or until time is called by the teacher. The team with the most points wins.

Strategy #7

Car Wash

Students line up in parallel lines about two to three feet apart. One or two students walk down the middle to receive a "wash" of compliment and/or affirmations.

Complimentary Car Wash

Jill has a sparkly personality.

What to Use

• no materials needed

What to Do

1. Discuss with students about giving and receiving compliments in an appropriate manner. It might be helpful to start with the "What I Like About You" activity (page 104).

2. Select one student at a time to be sent through the wash (between the lines), and in turn, those in the lines make round-and-round washing motions as they say words of praise, affirmation, or encouragement. You can have those in the lines shake the hand or pat the back of the student going through the wash. The pats on the back, handshaking, and verbal support produce a sparkling, shiny, happy "car" at the end of the wash!

3. Debrief both the "car" and the "washers" about how it felt to give and receive positive messages.

Notes for Success

• You may want to select only a few "washers" and let the rest of the class be observers who can participate in the debriefing at the end of the activity. (Another option is to select the "car" and have the car select its own washers.)

• Run one or two people through the car wash at a time rather than trying to do one big class clean-up. That insures that the responses of the washers are fresh, personal, and enthusiastic.

Ground rules

Compliments must be given directly to the "car" and said in first or second person using "I" or "You" to start the statement (no "he," "him," "her," or "she"). The "car" must remain silent. He or she must simply receive the compliment without any comment whatsoever.

Each "washer" must say something different about the "car." No repeats.

Strategy #8

Classroom Connect

This is an active classroom question-and-answer review game similar to "Connect Four™," using students as the game board.

What to Use

- review questions on individual index cards (one per student)
- 20 12-inch red circles
- 20 12-inch black circles

What to Do

1. Creating a human game board by placing 25 students in desks five rows across and five deep. Vary this arrangement with the number of students in your class. (You must have at least a four-by-four grid, and rows must be even.)
2. Give each of the students a question card and ask them not to show anyone.
3. Select two students to be the players.
4. Players stand at the front of the room.
5. One player gets the black disks, and the other gets the red disks.
6. Choose a player to go first.
7. That player chooses a student (on the first row horizontally).

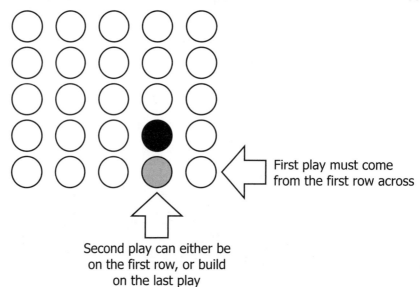

First play must come from the first row across

Second play can either be on the first row, or build on the last play

The Nuts & Bolts of Active Learning

8. The student selected reads the question card that she or he holds.

9. The player answers the question.
   - If the player is correct, he or she gives the student a colored circle.
   - If the player is incorrect, the correct answer is given, and the opposing player plays a colored circle.

10. The next player chooses a spot on the human play board. The player can choose any space on the first row across or build on colored circles already placed (similar to Connect Four game).

11. Play continues back and forth until a student places the fourth same-colored circle in a row (vertical, horizontal, or diagonal).

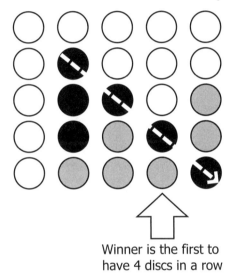

Winner is the first to
have 4 discs in a row

12. This player is the winner and stays for the next game. The losing player selects another student to play and takes that student's place on the human board.

13. The cards are taken up, shuffled, and redistributed to the students on the game board, or a different set of question cards are passed out.

Clock Partners

Students create a handy reference (a clock!) for predetermining 12 different partners they can meet with for collaborative work.

What to Use

- clock organizer (page 17) reproduced for individual students
- pencils

What to Do

1. Explain to students that they will be arranging 12 partner combinations for themselves—one for each hour on the clock. Pass out the clock organizers

2. When you give the signal, students will move about the room to locate partners for two-man teams. The two will exchange clocks and sign by the same hour. (Student A will sign Student B's clock on the line by three o'clock. Student B will sign Student A's clock on the line by three o'clock.)

3. Students repeat the process until they have found a partner for each hour of the day.

4. Have students store their clock organizers in a handy spot. Whenever you need a quick grouping by pairs, simply say, "Find your _____ o'clock partner and discuss _____."

Clock Partners

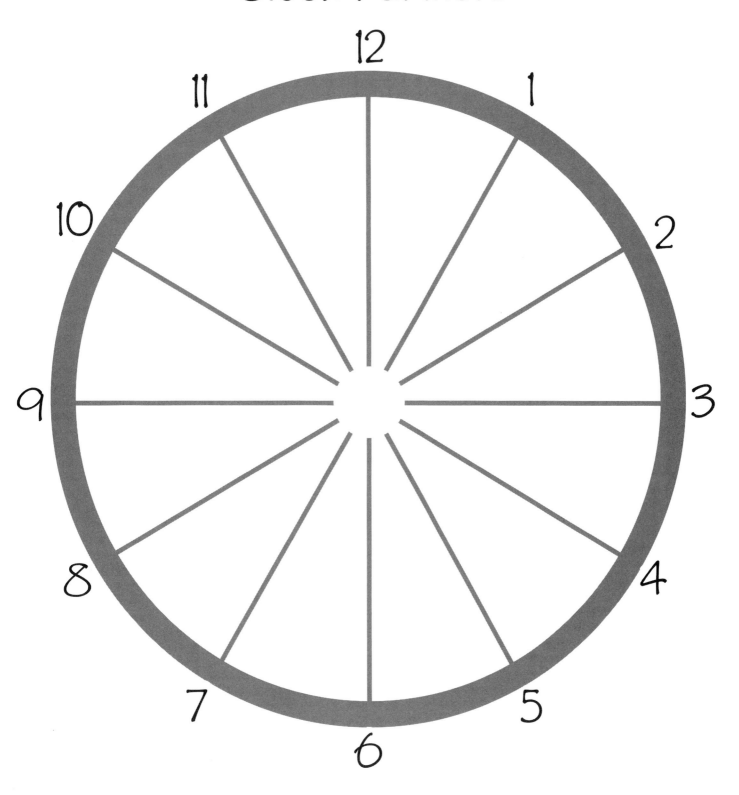

Collaborative Song Lyrics

A group of about 20 students follows a step-by-step approach to writing song lyrics. They explore effective writing through songwriting. The same process might be used to write an essay, a report, a poem, or a story.

And now for our next song title.

What to Use

- note cards or small rectangles of paper (several per student)
- masking tape
- sticky notes
- stopwatch

What to Do

1. Explain that the group will be writing a song (essay, poem, or story). Ask students to think about an intriguing title. You might use this scenario:

   Imagine you are listening to the radio and the announcer says, "Right after the break we'll be listening to the new hit: _____." Think of a title that would make you continue to listen through the commercial just to see what the song was about.
   Give students a two-minute period to think of a title. During this period no one talks. Students write their suggestions on a note card.

2. Have students tape the note cards to a display board so that the group can read them. (This is not a popularity contest, so the titles should be displayed without the names of their authors.) Have students read the list and "piggyback" on the suggestions. This is a second brainstorming time—students write any new title suggestions that are triggered by those already displayed and submit them for consideration.

3. The group chooses a title by voting on the one they want. Give every student five votes. If a student likes only one selection, he or she can give all five votes to that title. If a student likes more than one selection, he or she can divide up the votes between several different titles. One great way to do this voting is to give every student five sticky dots. Count the votes and announce the title. Remind students that unselected titles can become songs in the future.

4. This is another two-minute "no one talks" period. Have students write what a song with the new title might be about. For example, a song with the title "Nonsense" could be about silly rhymes, stereotypes, or a stern grandmother whose answer to any question is "Nonsense!" You get the idea. This step is all about determining the main idea.

5. As a group, come to some consensus about the main idea and then do another two-minute silent brainstorm period to think of details that support the main idea. In the example "Nonsense", if the group chose stereotypes, some of the details to emerge from this period might be "boys are better at math and they don't have manners" or "girls live at the mall and worry about their fingernails."

6. Now your group has a main idea and a list of possible details. You are ready to begin the actual writing. Practice collaboration as you write together. Remember: the lyrics do not have to rhyme. If you decide to have them rhyme, start with a phrase or main idea and brainstorm rhyming words at this point.

Nonsense

It doesn't work that way

That's not what all people do, not what all people say.

Those stereotypes and cliques are fiction.

Don't judge other people by their race or religion. Every label you can find

is your own defense

When you keep an open mind you avoid

Nonsense.

(from the song "nonsense" by Monte Selby and students in Scio, NY)

Strategy #11

Common Ground

Everyone thinks they are different and not like everyone else. This activity shows students that they share more than they think with their classmates, creating an atmosphere of acceptance. A wonderful activity for the first days of school or to use with an advisory group!

Nuts to the left, bolts to the right.

What to Use

- no materials needed

What to Do

1. Instruct students to group themselves around the room according to their answers to a question that you pose. The challenge is to do it without speaking or writing.

2. After each question, direct the follow-up question to a random student or two. Try asking students to reflect with someone else in the group.

3. Ask students to create and write down a grouping question as a follow-up.

4. Ask students to go back to their seats and write a reflection about what they learned from this activity and what surprised them most.

Strategy #12

Creative Candle Demonstration

Students are asked to write down observations and inferences about a common experience—watching a candle burn. However, there is a twist.

What to Use

- raw potato
- small candleholder
- sliver of an almond
- small knife
- matches

What to Do

1. Cut away all the peel of a small white potato. Trim the potato to look like a small votive candle or use a hollow pipe to create a "tapered" candle. Trim an almond sliver to fit inside the top of the "candle." Burn the tip of the almond for a more realistic appearance.

2. After you have discussed "going outside the lines" thinking with your students, tell them you want them to observe a common phenomenon and write down the most accurate description of what they actually see happening.

3. Stress that they are not to tell you what they expect the "right" answers to be. Simply make a list of observations (things they can know from their five senses).

4. Pull out a "candle" made of potato, apple, pear, or whatever you choose; its wick is made of some kind of nut sliver (the oil in it will burn just like a string wick).

5. Light it, turn out the classroom lights, and let it burn for about three minutes.

6. Have the children write down their observations, and then share them aloud with the class.

7. Accept all observations enthusiastically. Some will probably report seeing the wax melting, the sparks shooting out of the string, etc. Nod your head very attentively, thank them for their responses, then remind them that sometimes they need to think OUTSIDE the lines!

8. Begin eating the "candle" as you explain. Leave as the bell rings.

9. At the next class meeting ask students to "debrief" about the activity. Ask them to rethink their "observations." Stress the difference between observations and inferences.

Cross The Room

Students who disagree with each other meet together and discuss a particular topic.

What to Use

- no materials needed

What to Do

1. Divide the class in half and form two lines of students facing each other on opposite sides of the room. The teacher should then read a statement. Those students who DISAGREE with the statement should cross the room and join the opposite group, making certain to stand right next to someone who remained on their original side of the room. (Students will now end up in mixed opinion groups since only those students who disagreed with the statement crossed the room.)

2. Divide each large group into groups of four and assign a facilitator for each group.

3. The group discusses the topic, and students defend their positions. Each group should record their opinions on a large piece of paper labeled "FOR" and "AGAINST" and choose a spokesperson to report their opinions to the class.

4. Once all groups have shared, students should return to their seats and complete a writing assignment to be determined by the teacher.

Some possible questions might include:

a. How did you personally respond to the statement?

b. What was the most interesting thing you heard during your small group discussion? Why did you find it interesting?

c. What was the most interesting thing you heard during the whole class discussion? Why did you find it interesting?

d. After this discussion, was there anything that you heard to cause you to change your position? If so, what was it and who said it?

Dalderbash!

Students work in teams to try and test each other on word definitions or factual explanations. The person who is "it" reads the correct answer along with member-generated wrong answers. Individuals must decide which is the true answer. Students use "oral elaboration" (Robert Slavin, 1986) to discuss the ways they figured out the best responses.

What to Use

- reference materials
- list of questions or words
- several index cards or same-size small sheets of paper
- pencils or pens (same for everyone)

What to Do

1. Students are divided into four-member teams. One person on each team selects a question or a word from a list prepared by the teacher. (The words or questions should be things with which the students are not yet familiar.) He or she reads it aloud.

2. Each team member writes a possible definition of the word or an answer to the question on a piece of paper. The person with the reference book writes the real definition or explanation.

3. All the definitions or explanations are passed to the person holding the reference book. That person reads aloud all the answers, including the real one. Each player then has to try to guess the correct response.

4. A person scores one point if they guess the right answer. A person scores one point every time someone chooses his or her definition.

5. The job of "it" (reference book person) rotates through the team in whatever way the team decides.

6. Team members should debrief by talking about which people were most fooled by whom and why. Ask participants to tell each other what procedures they used to determine the correct response.

Dance the Answers

Music and rhythm help students remember what they have learned and ponder how to use it for answering questions.

What to Use

- dance music (interesting and appropriate to students)
- system for playing music
- large note cards

What to Do

1. Prepare a list of questions to use for reviewing a lesson or unit of study. Write one question on each side of each card. Create some questions that have the same answer as another question. You may repeat some of the questions on more than one card.

2. Prepare a list of corresponding answers.

3. Give each student a card. Allow a few minutes for students to ponder or even review material and think about the answers.

4. Students hold onto the cards and dance while you play music for a minute.

5. Stop the music and read an answer from your answer list.

6. Play music again. While the music is playing, any students who believe they have a question that matches the answer dance their way to the front of the room.

7. Stop the music and hear the questions that have emerged. Get quick agreement as to the accuracy.

8. Start the music again. Students turn over the card, and you read another answer. Continue the dance-question-dance answer sequence until you have reviewed the material.

Deal or No Deal

Representatives of student groups choose the question, scenario, or math problem that their group will solve.

What to Use

- index cards prepared in advance with scenarios, questions, problems, or readings

What to Do

1. Review collaborative procedures.
2. Divide students in small groups of three to five.
3. Have students pick one group representative
4. Spread out the index cards face down in a designated area.
5. Explain to students that the group representative will read the first card. The representative chooses that card for the group by responding, "Deal." If the representative does not want the card, he or she says, "No deal!" and must draw a second card. The "No deal!" option is available only for the first card picked.
6. Groups may repeat the choice procedure to do a second activity.
7. Allow time for reflection and group sharing.

 Strategy #17

Doodle to Remember

Brain research tells us that doodling or drawing helps us remember new information and concepts. So get students doodling to fix ideas into their memories.

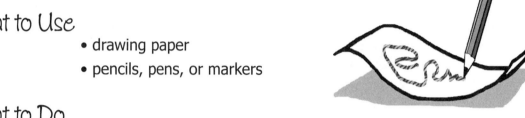

What to Use

- drawing paper
- pencils, pens, or markers

What to Do

1. Introduce a new concept, idea, process, or skill to students. Follow through with your usual procedure to discuss, practice, and extend this.

2. Give drawing paper to students.

3. Ask students to doodle or draw something that will help them remember the idea or process they have just learned.

4. After the doodling is done, gather students into small groups where they can show and explain their doodles.

Notes:

- Students will get better at this the more they do it. Give them many opportunities to doodle.

- YOU doodle, too. While they are drawing, do your own drawing to represent the new idea.

Explanation: When you divide a fraction by a fraction, you turn the second fraction upside down and multiply.

Strategy #18

Dot Buddies

Students quickly move into predetermined pairs to have a discussion, complete an assignment, or brainstorm solutions to a problem during a class period.

What to Use

- one 4 x 6 white index card for each student in the class
- one red, green, blue, and yellow adhesive dot for each student

What to Do

1. Before doing Dot Buddies for the first time, you will need to have students complete their Dot Buddies card. At the beginning of a class period, pass out cards so that each student has one card. Tell the students to walk around the room for a few minutes and find one different student to sign his or her name beside each dot on the card. For example, if I walk around the room looking for a person to sign by my red dot, I must find someone who also has a blank space by his or her red dot so we can both sign the same spot on the two cards.

2. Once all of the students have their dots signed, the students go back to their original seats.

3. Students write their own names on the back of their cards and put the dot cards aside.

4. Later during the class period, have the students to process some new information that was presented to them. Ask them to meet with their "red dot person" and complete an assignment, either written or verbal.

5. Later in the class, time permitting, assign some meeting time with blue dots, yellow dots, or green dots.

6. At the end of the class, collect the dot cards to be used another day.

> **Option:** Write a number on each card before the dot cards are distributed. Then since the index cards are also numbered, the teacher could call out a number and have that person share the results of their "red dot meeting" with the entire class. Call out a number of cards to spark a class discussion.

Strategy #19

Dream Team

Students identify, define, and then create qualities of a good working team.
Then they evaluate their own teamwork.

What to Use

- newspaper, magazines, Internet, and other reference materials
- chart paper and markers

What to Do

COOPERATE

offer input

BRAINSTORM

ideas

PLAN

compromise

task

DELEGATE

CONSENT

team work

1. Assign activity teams to discuss, research, record, and become a good working team.

   a. Divide class into small groups (teams).

   b. Groups brainstorm and use reference materials to create a list of situations that require a team. A time limit is set for writing down as many examples as possible. Suggest they think about the teamwork needed in sports, music, the theater, occupations, social events, businesses, and school. Responses should be written on the chart paper and displayed—Teamwork Required.

   c. If student groups have not included lists of situations in your school where teamwork is required, have them add these to their lists. If they have already included these situations, have them mark them with a star or circle them.

   d. Groups review their lists and create a new list of the qualities that are necessary for making a good working team—Qualities of a Successful Team.

   e. The groups then brainstorm examples of attitudes, actions, or incidents that can hinder a team's success possibilities—Behaviors That Interfere with Team Success.

2. Each group should be given time for critiquing its own success as a team.
   Did all participate?
   Was there discussion or arguing?
   Could roles be assigned?
   Was time used wisely?
   What could be done differently?
   Our team is successful because we . . .

> You may want to have groups evaluate their teamwork after each step, then they can "tweak" team actions as tasks are completed.

Strategy #20

Edible Academic Vocabulary

Students gain a practical understanding of five cross-disciplinary vocabulary terms when they DO the processes defined by those words. They'll have to do some eating in order to thoroughly practice the processes!

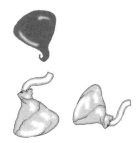

What to Use

- eight to ten groups of chocolate kisses in zip-lock bags (Each group should contain at least five different kinds, with wrappings that differ. Include no less than two or more of each kind in the bag.)
- pencil and note pad or paper for each group

What to Do

1. Divide students into groups of three or four. Give each group a bag of kisses, note pad, and pencil.

2. One at a time, define the terms. After discussing a term with students, give the instruction below that requires students to DO the process defined by the term. (Note: emphasize the difference between the terms, particularly between "arrange" or "classify" and "analyze" or "evaluate.")

ARRANGE: to place into a suitable order or relationship

Instruction: Arrange the kisses in some kind of order. Make notes or a diagram to describe the order.

CLASSIFY: to arrange in groups sharing at least one common attribute

Instruction: Agree on a system for classifying the kisses. Classify them and note a label for each class. Then, find a DIFFERENT way to classify the kisses. Do it, and note a label for each different classification system.

INFER: to derive (or surmise) as a conclusion from facts

Instruction: Without unwrapping the kisses, gather enough observations to make some inferences about what will be inside the wrapper. Make notes to briefly describe the inferences.

ANALYZE: to determine the nature and relationship of the parts

Instruction: Take actions and use your senses to analyze the kisses. List attributes and insights you gain from the analysis.

EVALUATE: to make a judgment; to decide the value or worth of

Instruction: Individually evaluate ONE of the kisses holistically. Make notes describing your judgments about the taste, satisfaction, appearance, smell, or other attributes that contribute to the whole. Note a summary statement of evaluation.

Strategy #21

Find Someone Who

This interactive activity can be used to review academic content.

What to Use

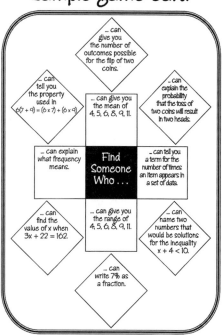

- "Find Someone Who" game card

  Example blocks:

  Find someone who can tell you what an acute triangle is and draw one in the block.

  Find someone who can tell you the three branches of government.

  Find someone who can name the stages of the water cycle.

  Find someone who knows what an antagonist is and can give you an example.

- a pen or pencil

What to Do

1. Provide each student with a "Find Someone Who" game card.

2. Each student is to find someone who can answer the review question in each block and have the person sign the block.

3. If a student can't remember what the person who knows the answer says, have them write the information in the block with the name.

4. Once students have completed the activity, go over the answers by calling on students whose names are in the blocks and see if other students agreed on their answers.

Strategy # 22

Fly on the Board

Students use fly swatters to choose the correct answer in an active review of information.

What to Use

- two fly swatters
- review questions

What to Do

1. Divide students into two groups.

2. Write four answer choices on the board.

3. A player from each team stands on opposites sides of the answers.

4. The players hold fly swatters at their sides.

5. Read a question.

6. The players each try to "swat" the correct answer first. The player who hits the right answer first gets a team point.

7. Another person from each team comes up, and a new question is read. (You may need to change the answer set.)

8. Play continues until teacher is ready for the closing "lightning round." Each team selects one player to play in the lightning round and decides how many points the team will wager. Note: the team can wager only up to the amount of the points they have earned, and the wager is kept a secret from the other team until after the lightning round is completed. One last question is read, and the players chosen respond with a "swat." The team's wagers are then revealed. If the player won, the points are awarded; if they lost, the points are deducted.

9. The winning team is the one with the most points.

Rules to Make It Easier
- Players can "swat" only one answer.
- If both players are wrong, two new players come up, and the next question is read.
- If only one player answers and answers incorrectly, the other player gets five seconds to try to answer the question.

Recognize Differences in the Way Directions Are Perceived

Fold It!

Students close their eyes and fold a paper according to oral directions. They compare papers and recognize that each understood the directions in a different, yet correct way.

What to Use

- one sheet of copy paper for each student

What to Do

1. Hand out one sheet of copy paper to each participant and ask everyone to listen closely and follow your directions precisely.

   Give these directions:

   - Hold your sheet of paper in front of you with both hands.
   - Close your eyes and do not open them again until I ask you to. Follow my exact directions, but ask no questions. Do not say anything until I ask you to open your eyes.
   - Fold your paper in half. (Pause)
   - Fold your paper in half again. (Pause)
   - Fold your paper in half again. (Pause)
   - Tear off the right-hand corner. (Pause)
   - Turn your paper over. (Pause)
   - Tear off the left-hand corner. (Pause)
   - Unfold your sheet of paper and hold it in front of you. (Pause)
   - Please open your eyes.

2. It will be immediately obvious that everyone does not have the same finished product. Discuss how individuals create understandings for themselves in different ways.

3. Apply this demonstration to individual differences in the classroom.

The Nuts & Bolts of Active Learning

Strategy #24

Formal Outfit Wrap

Students work in teams to create "formal outfits" out of an unlikely material. This is a great activity for Spirit Day, Mardi Gras, Homecoming, or other special school occasions.

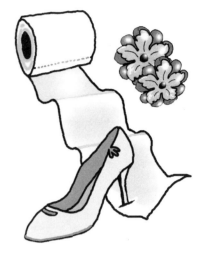

What to Use

- computer and LCD projector (optional)
- rolls of toilet paper • tape • straight pins
- safety pins • scissors • rubber bands

What to Do

1. Show the students pictures from this website without the title or identifying captions:
   www.cheap-chic-weddings.com/wedding-contest-2006.html

2. Ask students if they see any unusual similarities among the dresses. List all that they cite. If no one guesses, tell them that all the dresses are made of toilet paper.

3. Tell each team they are going to design, create, and provide a model for a piece of "formal apparel" (tux or gown). The team must be prepared to explain the unique features and outstanding qualities of their creation.

4. Gowns and tuxes must be created by using only toilet paper as the outfit material. Tape, pins, and rubber bands may be used for purposes of fitting and special effects, but they should not be visible. All decorative accessories must also be made of toilet paper.

5. Gowns must be substantial enough to remain intact throughout the modeling portion of the contest.

6. Gowns or tuxes can be worn over regular school clothing, body suits, or swimsuits. The school's dress code policy should not be violated by the fashion show.

7. Gowns and tuxes will be judged on:
   adherence to the rules of the contest, adherence to the dress code, teamwork, aesthetic quality, artistry, creativity, utlity, narration

   Judging can be done by an outside guest, the teacher, the other groups, a group self-evaluation, or a combination of these.

8. This is a fun activity that can be enhanced by catwalk music, cheap plastic trophies (or other garish prizes), photo opportunities, acceptance speeches, etc.

9. Questions to debrief:

   a. How did your team work together to solve the problem of creating a unique prom dress (tux)?

   b. What could your team have done to improve your results?

   c. Would you have been better able to do this activity alone? Why or why not?

   d. What are some of the positive aspects of working together on a team project?

   e. What are some of the drawbacks of working together on a team project?

   f. Do you think the judging criteria is fair? Why or why not?

   g. Rather than waste the toilet paper we used in these creations, what could we do with it that would be environmentally sound? (Examples: use it for packing material; reroll it and use it as you would any tissue paper.)

Extension Activities:

- Put on the fashion show for an elementary class, or film it for YouTube.com or to show in a nursing home or hospital room.

- Write an essay describing how the world would be affected if, by tomorrow, everyone on the planet wore the same style, cut, type, and color of clothing.

- Write a journal page from the perspective of a Goth, Emo, Whale-tail, or other extreme dresser. Explain why dressing that way is important to you.

Strategy #25

From the Heart

Students seated in a circle are given the opportunity to express their feelings about a statement or situation. Cooperation is reinforced through the sharing of individual feelings and the practice of listening skills.

What to Use

- large stuffed heart, bear, or other plush toy

What to Do

1. The leader sits with students in a circle (either on the floor or in chairs).

2. Participants take turns sharing their feelings or ideas on a topic as they hold the stuffed animal.

3. When the student is finished, he or she passes the stuffed animal on to the next person. This continues until everyone has had the opportunity to share. The leader also shares but is careful not to dominate the activity.

4. Generally it is best to start students with "safe" subjects such as:

    I like it when . . .
    My favorite thing to do is . . .
    My favorite quality in a person is . . .
    I am happy when . . .

> Subjects of more depth can be explored once participants build trust among one another and become more comfortable with the activity.

Ground Rules

- Only the participant with the stuffed animal may talk. Everyone else actively listens and supports the person who is speaking.

- A participant ALWAYS has the right to pass and give the stuffed toy to the next person.

- Anything shared in this activity is PRIVATE!!! Participants should be aware that nothing communicated during "From The Heart" can be told outside the group. Everything must be held in confidence.

- No one participant should monopolize the activity. Students should be sure that everyone gets a turn.

- Participants should talk only about what they feel, not about how others in the group feel.

Strategy #26

Gallery Walk

Groups of students rotate among posters with questions and create a consensus response. The Gallery Walk is an assessment that capitalizes on the "people smart" intelligence. It can be used as a diagnostic, formative, or summative assessment.

What to Use

- large poster paper or chart paper
- tape
- markers

Describe something structural about a zebra that would hinder its ability to survive at the North Pole. Tell why.

What to Do

1. The teacher poses challenge questions for students to answer in small groups (two to five participants). Student groups rotate among the questions written on large pieces of newsprint or giant poster paper placed around the room. Each group has a different-colored felt-tip marker. They write one answer on each poster. Answers cannot be duplicated.

2. The teacher gives the groups a set amount of time to read the question, read the answers already written (after the first round), and generate a new answer that demonstrates their understanding of the concept.

3. After the rotations are finished, all posters are brought to the front of the room so that the answers can be discussed and evaluated.

4. Later the teacher can make a formative assessment of each group's contribution to the overall activity because each group responded with a different colored marker.

- A nuclear holocaust has impacted the world. The only human survivors have been forced to live underground deep within the earth. They can never come out to the earth's surface again. What kind of structural adaptations in the population could you expect to find over time? Why?

- Describe something structural about a zebra that would hinder its ability to survive at the North Pole. Tell why.

- Describe a behavioral adaptation a cat might try in order to have a chance of successfully living with a pack of dogs.

- Imagine that you are a bright orange butterfly. A predator that preys on bright orange butterflies moves into your habitat. What could you do so that the population of bright orange butterflies survives?

- You are a fox who preys on the mice living on the island where you live. Suddenly the mice have developed the ability to swim, and you are having trouble catching enough food to survive.
  Describe a behavioral or structural adaptation that might help you solve your problem.

- Describe a behavioral adaptation a fifth grader will need to make in order to "fit in" at the middle school next year.

Getting-to-Know-You BINGO

Get acquainted and learn some things about each other with this variation on an old favorite game.

What to Use

- list of all student names on board
- nine-inch squares of poster board
- marking pens
- pennies or paper clips or other bingo markers for each student
- notepad and pencil

What to Do

1. Prepare poster board BINGO cards as shown. (Note: Use 6 x 6 squares and write the word UNIQUE instead of BINGO. Give one to each student.

2. Give students a few minutes to think about something they would like the group to know about themselves—an interest, hobby, skill, characteristic, or other important bit of information.

3. While students are thinking, they create their BINGO boards by writing the first name and initial of the last name of a student in each square. (They find the names on the board.)

4. Students take turns presenting themselves: Each student circles his or her name on the board and tells the class, briefly, one thing about himself or herself.

5. As students introduce themselves, the teacher makes note of the special things they tell about themselves.

6. Read items from the list, one at a time. Students put a marker on the name that connects to the characteristic.

7. The game continues until someone cries out, "BINGO!" Check to see if the card is correct.

Grab It! Show It!

When students reach into the grab bag, they have no idea what concept will be drawn out. But whatever it is, they will do some action, or role-play in some way to SHOW the concept, using few or no props.

What to Use

- small shopping bag or basket
- index cards
- timer

What to Do

1. Identify key concepts, ideas, or terms from a unit of study.
2. Write each of these on paper. Place them in the bag or basket.
3. Students work in small groups. Each group draws a card.
4. Set the timer for five minutes. Group members decide how they will show (demonstrate) the term or concept.
5. Groups take turns demonstrating.
6. If the class knows what the concept is, other students make notes about what the group does to show the concept well.
7. If you choose for the class NOT to know the concept ahead of time, other students may make guesses about what concept is being demonstrated.

Samples Ideas (from Many Subject Areas)

alliance	inertia	phototropism
philanthropy	symbiosis	distributive property
diplomacy	catalyst	immune
insulator	merger	ratio
trapezoid	pointillism	legato
staccato	thespian	ligament
populism	reciprocal	imperialism
equilibrium	square root	positive slope
conjunction	analogy	parenthesis

Highlight Training Video

Students videotape the way classroom procedures are supposed to look. For example, imagine a video showing the appropriate way to enter the classroom, turn in papers, and begin bell work. Think highlight videos that are taken of the football game to help players visualize the proper offense and defense.

A Day in the Life of Garfield School

a Grade 7 production

What to Use

- video camera
- students

What to Do

1. Designate a team of students who will videotape "the way it should look" examples of classroom and hallway procedures. If students need instruction on operating the equipment, make sure that they have it. Have students practice videotaping to make sure they are ready for action.

2. You may choose to set up a scenario to videotape or have your videotape crew ready to capture the spontaneous actions of students.

3. Watch the video together and point out the positives.

4. Repeat videotaping and watch again.

5. Celebrate the improvement you see.

> **Note:** Create a video at the end of the year to show during the upcoming year.

Strategy #30

Hot Seat

Students answer questions about themselves by changing seats with those who share common attributes.

What to Use

- one chair per student, less one

What to Do

1. Provide one seat for every student except for the student designated as "It."

2. "It" stands and calls out a description of an attribute that he or she has, such as:

   "Everyone who has ever been tardy for this class . . . "

   "Anyone who has a cat . . . "

   "People who have ever cut their own hair and made a terrible mistake . . ."

   "Everyone who has ever been to California . . ."

3. Everyone (including "It") who matches the description must jump up and change seats with others who match the description.

4. "It" grabs an empty seat.

5. The person who is left over becomes "It," and the game starts again.

This is a great energizer when students are tired or not focused.

 *Strategy #31*

Human Machines

Groups of students will work together to become a machine. Each member of the group has to become a component, other groups try to guess the machine being demonstrated.

What to Use

- no materials needed

What to Do

1. Ask the whole class to brainstorm types of machines that are used every day.

2. Explain to the class that they are going to work in small groups to create human models of actual machines. They can bring to life one of the machines from the class brainstorm list or another one that the group agrees on.

3. They'll have to decide what machine they'll create and how they act it out.

4. Divide the class into groups of four to six people.

5. Give groups five to eight minutes to choose a machine and practice their presentation. Each member must be a component of the machine.

6. Each group presents a performance of their machine, and the class guesses what machine they represent.

7. (optional) Have the class vote on the "best" machine.

Example: Toaster

One student is the lever. When it goes down another person (toast) drops down, two other people stand on each side of the "toast" heating it. When finished, the toast and the lever POP UP and the heaters stop heating!

Human Maps

Students actually use their own bodies to show the correct location of places, events, or other elements on a "map" of a system.

What to Use

- cards or paper and markers
- pins or string and hole punch
- large paper for map background
- masking tape

Examples of Systems that Can Be Mapped

- interrogative sentence
- solar system
- teeth in the human bopdy
- components of the skeletal system
- world continents or bodies of water
- countries in Africa
- U.S. states in the northeastern region
- components of a geometric shape
- atoms in a molecule
- ideas in a planning web
- components in a graphic organizer
- topic sentences of paragraphs in an essay
- words in a sentence
- terms in an equation

What to Do

1. Clarify the content that students need to reinforce with the human map.

2. If a background is needed (such as an outline of a country, a web, a drawing of the upper and lower jaw areas, or a circle with divisions for a graphic organizer), prepare this on a large sheet of paper. Boundaries and divisions can also be marked on the floor with masking tape.

3. Identify the elements that will be on the map (for example: names of mountain ranges, names of countries, labels for writing web sections, sentences for a paragraph, or individual terms for an equation). Direct students as they help by making labels for the elements.

4. Give a label to each student. These can be pinned to shirts or attached to string and worn around the neck.

5. Direct students to take their places on the map. They can gauge their places by taking the right spot on the background. If there is no background, they will need to place themselves in relation to the other elements.

The Human Slide Rule

This activity is a variation of Four Corners, but the participants SLIDE down a line to meet with a person of a differing opinion.

What to Use

- two poster board signs—STRONGLY AGREE and STRONGLY DISAGREE

What to Do

1. Make a controversial, black-and-white statement about a topic learned in school or something that has happened in the school, community, country, or world.

2. Allow the students a few minutes to think about their response to this question.

3. Place the two signs on opposite sides of the room. Ask the students to line themselves up in a straight line according to how they feel about the statement, ranging from STRONGLY AGREE to STRONGLY DISAGREE.

4. Split the line in half. One half takes a step forward, turns around, and SLIDES down the line until they are positioned directly opposite the students from the other half of the line. Students who STRONGLY AGREE with the statement will now be facing others who are somewhat neutral. Students who STRONGLY DISAGREE with the statement will also be facing relatively neutral peers.

5. Once everyone is in position, tell students that one of the pair will be a dog and one will be a cat. The students in the individual pairs should choose. Ask to hear from the dogs and the students will automatically bark. Then, we must hear from the cats. Of course, the cats will then meow.

6. Once the characters in the pairs have been determined, ask that the cat go first and share their opinion with their dog. Then, the dog must share. The total dialogue should only last about four minutes.

7. Call upon three or four pairs to share their responses with the entire class.

8. After the brief sharing session, the group that slid down the line should slide down the line back to their original positions.

9. The line will now fold completely in half so that the STRONGLY AGREE students will now be paired up with the STRONGLY DISAGREE students and the more neutral folks will be paired up together.

10. Once the students are in their new pairs, have students designate one in the pair as a monkey and one as a lion. Once again, the individual pairs decide this. As before, ask to hear first from the monkeys and then from the lions.

11. The monkeys should go first to state their case, and then the lions should follow. The total time for dialog is about four minutes. At this point, tell the students that they will be stating their partner's opinion — not their own, so they must listen closely.

12. This time, when a pair is called upon to share with the entire class, a student (monkey or lion) must state the case of the OTHER student in their pair, and then the remaining partner must state the opposite partner's view as well. This encourages all students to actively listen to their partners.

13. Once a few partners have been heard from, the students should return back to their original seats and complete a brief writing assignment. Some possible questions are:
    a What is the most interesting thing that you heard today from your partner OR someone else?
    b Why did you find it interesting?
    c Who made the statement?
    d Did you hear anything today that caused you to rethink your position and change your mind? If so, what was it that you heard?

14. This written assignment could be turned in for written comments OR could merely be an entry in their class journals.

Strategy #34

Hunker Hauser

In this summer camp favorite, two students participate in a nontraditional tug-of-war where a strategy of taking risks can lead to success.

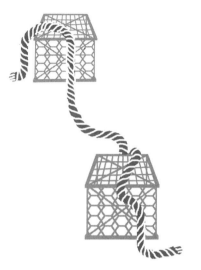

What to Use

- two milk crates
- 100-foot rope
- two pair of garden gloves
- grass or carpeted area

Note: Do not place milk crates on linoleum or tile flooring, as the crates may slip while students are standing on them.

What to Do

1. Place two milk crates on grass or carpet about 40 to 50 feet apart.

2. Two students put on garden gloves and each stands on a crate.

3. Hand the ends of the rope to the students. The students adjust the rope so the excess rope has collected behind them and they are holding a fairly taut line between themselves.

4. Challenge students to do whatever it takes to get their competitor either to drop the rope or to step off the crate. Whoever remains standing on the crate with the rope in hand wins.

> **Note:** To get his or her competitor to make a mistake, a player may have to employ a series of actions that consist of alternately gripping the rope, then releasing it so it slides freely between his or her hands before it is gripped again. Smaller students can beat larger students at this if they unbalance their opponents by alternate gripping and loosening of the rope.

5. Once students have had some fun with this activity, ask them to pause for a moment and look for metaphors within the fun.

   - Are there times when we have more advantage by letting go of something?

   - Are there times when we need to hold onto something? Is either of these a risky choice for us? If so, in what way?

Strategy #35

The "I CAN"

Students use cans to "store" and show off what they have learned. Each student's can accumulates things they know and can do. Periodically they will be asked to demonstrate that they really CAN do the things in the I CAN!

What to Use

- empty, clean, aluminum cans with one end removed
- paper, markers, glue, crayons, scissors, and decorations for cans
- ample supply of paper strips for writing accomplishments

What to Do

1. Explain that the can is a place for recording and celebrating what they can do. It is also a tool for repeating, reviewing, and strengthening those skills. This means that someone may draw a slip from the can and ask them to SHOW that they, indeed, CAN do that skill, or that they do know that concept.

> Explain the concept of the I CAN this way: When you learn a new skill or master a concept, you write it on a slip of paper. Write it in the form of what you can do or show: "I can_____." Celebrate what you CAN do by putting that slip into your I CAN.

2. Provide time and supplies for each student to create an I CAN.
3. Provide paper slips. Each time a student masters a skill, provide reminders to add that to the I CAN.
4. Periodically, ask each student to draw a slip from the I CAN to demonstrate that knowledge or skill.

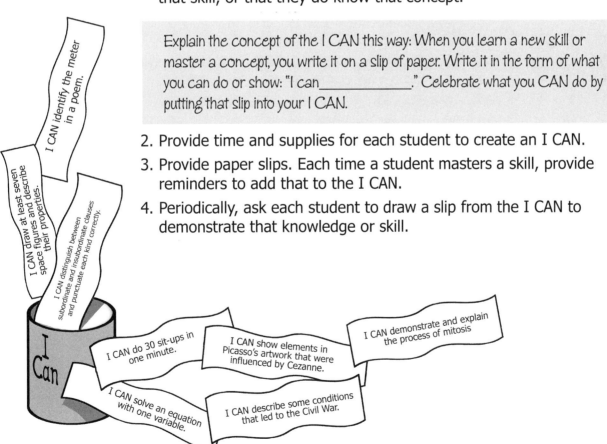

I CAN identify the meter in a poem.

I CAN draw at least seven space figures and describe their properties.

I CAN distinguish between subordinate and insubordinate clauses and punctuate each kind correctly.

I CAN do 30 sit-ups in one minute.

I CAN show elements in Picasso's artwork that were influenced by Cezanne.

I CAN demonstrate and explain the process of mitosis

I CAN solve an equation with one variable.

I CAN describe some conditions that led to the Civil War.

Strategy #36

Impromptu Speeches

An "impromptu speech" is a speech given with little or no preparation. This activity requires each student to choose a random topic, prepare for one to two minutes, and give an impromptu speech for the class.

What to Use

- list of topics, cut up
- copies of student procedures and rubrics
- blank note card for each student

Before the Activity

1. Prepare a jar containing small slips of paper with a variety of topics on them (suggestions below). The topics need to be very general so students can improvise based on their own knowledge.

2. Copy and distribute the student procedures and evaluation sheet and review the "tips for success."

3. Call one student at a time to speak. It works well to have one student speaking while the next one is in the hall getting ready; that way each student has one to two minutes to prepare, and there is no long pause between speeches.

Step by Step for Student

1. When your turn is called, choose a topic out of the jar. If you don't want that topic, you get one refusal; but then you MUST use the second one you choose. Give the teacher your evaluation sheet to use while you speak.

2. You will have one to two minutes to prepare your speech and you may use one note card. (See the tips below for help with this step.)

3. When it's time for you to start, there will be a student timer to help you. To receive an A, your speech needs to last from 60 to 90 seconds.

Tips for Success

- Think BIG! Instead of discussing specific details first, think about big topics that you can discuss for a while.

- Expand your thinking about the topic so you can talk about what you know. For example, if you draw "goldfish," you could talk about fish, pets, crackers, etc. If you draw "movies," you could talk about what they are, how they're made, or the best one you ever saw.

- Practice! While you won't be able to practice your exact topic, you can work on technique. To do this, find a partner and have him or her give you a random topic. Take one to two minutes to jot down your ideas, and then give your "speech." Have your partner time you and give you tips when you're done. This will only be helpful if you pretend like it's the real thing — no stopping and starting once you've begun.

Ideas for topics

money	hair	friends	homework
school lunches	the mall	fingernails	pets
movies	weather	pizza	cell phones
football	rocks	birthdays	music
summer jobs	Valentine's Day	swimming	

*Note: This activity can be easily adapted to be an assessment for a specific subject area. For example, if students have just finished a study of the American Revolution, topics might include the Boston Tea Party, Stamp Act, Declaration of Independence, and Continental Congress,.

Strategy #37

This space available

"It's All Me" Design, Inc.

Students create a T-shirt design and share designs in the classroom so that classmates and teachers can build relationships.

What to Use

- 11" x 16" sheets of paper cut to a T-Shirt shape
- markers
- clothesline
- clothespins

What to Do

1. Explain to students that they are the lead designers in their own T-Shirt design company. Have them think about different styles of T-shirts and how each design reflects something different. As the lead designers, they need to design their own T-shirts that reflect their values, dreams, and personality.

   You may want to take time to

   - Talk to students about values. Brainstorm a class list of values that people have.
   - Talk to students about goals and dreams. Share how goals are not always materialistic. Talk about how goals and dreams can be different based on the timeline

   Have students write three goals that they want to accomplish.

   - Talk to students about personalities and how different people have different personality traits.
   - Have students create a cluster map describing how these areas relate to their own personality, values, and goals/dreams.

2. Students sketch out the design on regular paper and then transfer the final design to the T-shirt templates. As they finish the design, they hang the T-shirt on the clothesline that is hung around the room.

3. As an evaluation, students can develop and use a rubric to evaluate each of the designs posted around the room. Rubric categories might include:
   - values identified
   - personality
   - T-shirt's "sell-ability" rated on a scale of one to ten stars
   - goals and dreams
   - best thing about a shirt

4. (optional) Give "top design" awards to the shirts.

Strategy #38

Junk Drawer Wrap-Up

The wrap-up from a lesson (or unit) is crucial to solidifying concepts learned. In this activity, students restate and summarize main ideas by connecting them to selected throw-away items.

What to Use

- a collection of (clean) items from the junk drawer
- large note cards, pens, or pencils
- baskets (one for each small group)

What to Do

1. Put an assortment of junk items into each basket.
2. Prepare questions or topics pertaining to the big ideas from a unit of study. Write each of these on a note card.
3. Divide students into small groups. Give each group a basket of junk items and a few of the prepared note cards.
4. The basket is passed in the group. Each student takes an item that they can connect in some way to the topic or that they can use to answer the question.
5. After students have had a few minutes to think, they take turns telling the group why they chose the item.
6. Items are returned to the basket.
7. As time permits, more cards are drawn, and the process (5–7) is repeated.

Killer Statements and Gestures

In this activity, students explore words and actions that "kill" the spirit of others.

What to Use

- chart paper or poster board
- glue or glue sticks
- markers
- paper
- scissors
- magazines

What to Do

1. Conduct a class discussion around the following questions:

   a. Have you ever worked really hard at something or been very excited about something and someone "killed" your good feeling by something they said or did? What was said or done?

   b. Have you ever witnessed someone's pride or other feelings being "killed" by something that someone else said or did? What was said or done? How do you think the other person felt?

2. Introduce the concept of "killer statements and gestures" as anything that is said or done to "kill" someone's good feelings about themselves. These things can be negative comments, body language, or gestures.

3. List together some of the things that are often said in and around the classroom that fit these categories (even those said and done by staff members).

   Examples may include:
   "That doesn't even make sense!"
   "Where did you get an answer like that?"
   "Quit showing off!"
   "Are you crazy? retarded? weird? strange? nuts? . . ."
   "We don't have time for that now."
   "Only boys/girls do that!"
   "If you'd pay attention, this wouldn't happen!"

4. Tell the students to keep a list of all the killer statements they hear throughout the day. Discuss who said them and why.

5. Have students make a mural or collage of killer statements and gestures. They can create pictures and word strips and/or cut out examples from magazines. Display in the room as a reminder.

6. Discuss how to replace killer statements and gestures with positive comments and gestures.

Strategy #40

Improve Cooperation and Collaboration

Our logo turned out great!

Learning Squad Detectives

Learning Squad Formation

Students work in small groups of students to begin to form a cohesive unit.

What to Use

- student worksheet (1 copy per group)
- colored pencils or markers
- poster paper (optional)

What to Do

1. Divide class into small groups.
2. Distribute student worksheet to group.
3. Set a time limit and have students work as a group to fill in the worksheet.

Learning Squads

List the names (first and last) of the people in your squad: _____

_____

_____

In the space below, brainstorm possible names for your squad. _____

_____

Now choose a name you can all live with for the next few weeks and write it on the line.

_____

In the space to the right, list at least three rules your squad can agree on that will be in effect whenever you work together: _____

_____

Now come up with three goals your squad has. At least one should be related to working together and getting along, and at least one should be related to completing your work. _____

_____

In the box on this page, design a colorful logo for your squad. It can look like anything you want (appropriate, of course!). This will be your "rough draft." You will be making a poster of this design after it's approved.

Your next task is to come up with a way to introduce your squad to the class. You may make up a rap, a song, a cheer, or a short skit. Plan below, and be sure to include your squad's name in your introduction! _____

_____

_____

_____

_____

_____

Let's Get Physical with Writing!

Students add sentences to each others' stories while they are the stories on their backs and they work collaboratively to edit and publish a group story.

What to Use (for each student)

- one file folder
- one washable felt tip pen
- one piece of masking tape about a foot long

What to Do

Part One—A Large Group Activity

1. Tell students to open their file folders to form one long sheet. They will write a beginning line or phrase that might start a story at the very top of the open folder. But before they write their sentence or phrase, explain several things:

   - The line does not have to be a complete sentence, although it can be as long as they would like it to be.

   - Spelling does not count during the first part of this activity.

2. Then model several examples of what a starter phrase might be. Write them on the board or project them overhead.

   - Consider something classic such as: "It was a dark and stormy night . . . " or "Once upon a time in a land far, far away . . .".

   - Consider the beginning of a horror story such as: "The girl screamed as the bloody head rolled by!" or "They heard the scream come from the dark woods."

   - Students might have some fun at your expense with, "It was a normal day in Mr. T's class when suddenly . . .". Provide several examples and make sure the students know that they can copy one of the examples, or they can make up one of their own.

3. Ask the students to write their beginning phrase or sentence. Have several folders prepared with a story starter already written on the top and offer them to students who might be hesitant to write on their own.

> Note: Have the room already set up for this activity so that you can begin the introduction and implementation with the students and not get bogged down with the logistics. Tear off enough pieces of tape and

place them around the classroom so that students can get to them easily. Sticking them to the wall in various places around the room works well. Have a file folder and felt tip pen on each desk, or have students pick them up as they enter the classroom. When you have materials all ready for the students as they come in, you have already taken away excuse number one for not participating. Take away any other excuses a student might have for not doing this writing activity by following these simple directions.

4. Have students locate pieces of tape that you have positioned around the room. They tear the tape in half and put it on the corners of their file folders. Then they position the file folders over their shoulders, holding them in place with the tape. Remind them that the activity will work infinitely better if they position the file folder on their back so that the starter phrase is facing outward. In essence they are going to become walking billboards.

5. Now students move around the room and get at least 10 to 15 other students (about half of the students in your class) to add to their stories. As they add to each other's stories remind them of these guidelines:
   • They do not have to add complete sentences.
   • They can add just a few words, or they can add a paragraph.
   • They may try to follow the story line that is there, or they may feel free to take the stories in any direction they want as they add a line. (Sometimes students get stuck on a story and truly do not know where to go with it. If they find themselves in that position, they simply can add the words "and then . . . ," and move on to another story.
   • The last student to add a line to a story does not have to bring the story to a conclusion. The students should just add another phrase to keep the story going.

6. After students have the required number of lines on their stories, they may take off the file folders and return to their seats to read and enjoy the bizarre stories the class has written.

7. Each student has the beginnings of a story. All of the folders look equally bad or good with all kinds of handwriting, and the stories are all over the place. You may want to share a few of the stories at this point. Each student has no responsibility for what his or her story sounds like since it was written by a number of other students.

1. Divide the class into teams of five or six. It is important to be very careful to create diverse teams.

2. Each member of a team reads his or her story to the team. Again it is important to remind students that they are not at all responsible for what has been written on their placards. They also need to know that all of the stories will be difficult to read since most of the handwriting is poor due to difficult writing conditions. After each student has had the chance to share his or her story, the team must choose one of the stories it would like to revise and successfully conclude. The revised story will be read to the class.

3. When each team decides on one of the stories and how it should end, one member of the team will write that ending on the placard. The team will also select a designated reader. When all of the teams have finished, the reader will read the team's story to the rest of the class.

4. Each team will present the story it has completed.

Making Connections:

1. Ask each team why they picked the story they chose to complete and share, and why some of the others were more difficult to use.

2. Record what the students say. You will hear things like: "some of the stories did not have a beginning, middle, and end'; 'some of the stories did not get our attention'; 'some of the stories had too many incomplete sentences'; and so on. Facilitate this discussion so that the students describe what they did to their stories and actually define how to write a good narrative story.

3. Now ask each team to go back and review all of the stories in its team. As a team they are to suggest possible ways to edit and provide endings to complete the rest of the stories. Again, it is not always the gifted writers that offer the better suggestions. Everyone seems willing to offer opinions about how the stories could be improved and completed.

Everyone came to the going-away party ~~eccept~~ except Theo. He was still ~~angery~~ angry at ~~d~~ Donna's sister for calling him dumb.

4. Each student in the team then takes his or her story with the suggested edits and endings and begins the editing process.

Part Three—The Individual Activity

1. Individuals may follow the team's suggestions or they may make their own edits as they work on their stories. Remind them to follow the guidelines that you recorded earlier. Students may or may not change the storyline on their folders.

2. Process student progress with their stories. Ask questions such as:
   • What difficulties have you had making corrections?
   • What is the most common problem on the folder?

   As the students share their experiences, they will again directly or indirectly address good sentence structure, follow a train of thought, develop topic sentences, and think about the differences between narrative and descriptive paragraphs. As they describe what they were trying to do with their stories, facilitate the discussion and relate the appropriate terminology.

3. Have the students go back and forth a few more times to help each other with the stories. Continue to facilitate their discussions as they learn about the form and structure that make a quality piece of writing.

Strategy #42

Living Tableau

Students pose as a frozen scene that depicts a concept, theme, or narrative.

What to Use

- open space

What to Do

1. Choose the story, text, or concept that students will depict visually.

2. Identify central concepts or events that are crucial to understanding the whole idea. As a whole group, pick out four to six "scenes" that you feel summarize the concept or text. (The number may vary depending on the topic.)

3. Decide on the characters (forces or ideas), setting, and other details that need to be visually communicated. Write or describe what each scene should communicate. Determine what the characters (forces or ideas) will do visually to depict the important details, emotions, aspects, and significance of what you are presenting.

4. Create, act out, and freeze the scenes or mental models into tableau. Students will imagine that they were suddenly made into statues at the high point or most illuminating juncture of their depiction.

5. Melt the first tableau and reform it into another one that captures the next event or key detail. Repeat until all tableaux have been created. Have students work in groups to consider how to present the series of scenes in a way that communicates the important details.

6. Rehearse and perform. The complete presentation should be about three minutes.

The Luck of the Draw

Cartoons inspire students to review and broaden key terms, processes, and ideas.

What to Use

- collection of cartoons or other drawings
- a large box with a slit cut in the top
- pencils or fine-point marking pens
- review sheet from lesson or unit of study (student notes about key terms, ideas, and processes learned)

What to Do

1. Copy cartoons or drawings. Remove any captions. Also, remove any words from talk balloons within cartoons.
2. Fold papers and place them in a box.
3. Make sure students have a list or summary of key terms or concepts for review and extension.
4. Each student (or pair of students) draws a paper from the box.
5. Give this direction: Write a caption for the cartoon or write the words in the talk balloons or thought bubbles in a way that teaches, uses, explains, or applies one of the key concepts.
6. Students (or pairs) exchange completed cartoons with other students and discuss or explain their work.

Megapuzzles

Large graphic organizers are completed and cut apart to make puzzles. Puzzle pieces are shuffled before students work together in groups to put all the puzzles back together.

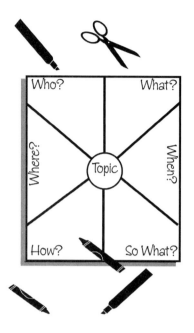

What to Use

- large pieces of poster board
- compass and meter stick
- marking pens
- several pairs of scissors
- list of topics or events from a unit of study

What to Do

1. Prepare several identical pieces of poster board, each laid out as a blank graphic organizer. Draw a circle in the center and lines to divide the remaining space into six equal wedges.

2. Write a topic in the circle on each poster.

3. Label the six sections: What? Who? When? Where? How? and So What?

4. Divide students into small groups. Give each group a piece of poster board, marking pens, scissors, and the label of one of the topics.

5. Students write the topic in the center circle (using large print). They fill in the graphic organizer with information (words, phrases, sentences) that answers the questions.

6. Students cut completed organizers apart, leaving a circle and six wedges.

7. Take all the pieces and mix them up. Lay the circles out all over the floor in an open space. Put the wedge pieces in a big pile.

8. Each group "draws" six random wedges from the pile. Then groups work to put the organizers back together. They must use the information on the wedges to decide where each one belongs.

Mission Statements

Students learn about missions statements and then create one for their class.

MISSION STATEMENT
Accepting the challenge of tomorrow, our mission is to create a nurturing, learning environment where we reach for and realize our potential.

Because students of today face a different kind of tomorrow, we believe these things are essential for learning:

Positive Self Esteem
Confidence, courage and responsible risk taking
Problem solving and creative thinking
Expectations of excellence

What to Use

- school history, profile, and policy information
- computer Internet connection or reference access to community organizations
- paper and pencil

What to Do

1. Appoint a committee to define "mission statement" and identify the components of a good mission statement — purpose, population, responsibilities, product or services offered. (This is a great opportunity to use the Internet, but other reference materials can also be used.)

2. Assign teams to find examples of mission statements. Suggest the teams explore Internet sites for colleges, nonprofit, and large organizations, such as: the University of Tennessee, Ford Motor Company, Goodwill Industries, Boy Scouts of America.

3. Appoint a committee to go to the office to find the mission statement for the school and bring a copy back for class discussion. (This would be an opportunity for a school administrator to participate in your classroom.)

4. Have each committee (team) to share their findings. Compare the statements and identify mission statement components in each. How are the statements alike? How are they different?

5. Encourage "feedback" from all the students.

6. Create a mission statement for your class and post it in the room and outside of the classroom door.

*Remember that, generally, shorter mission statements are more effective than longer ones.

Students may want to compose their own personal mission statements.

Strategy #46

Name That Student

Students try to match information about people in their class with the correct names of the persons being described.

What to Use

- note cards
- handouts

I love football and track.

What to Do

I am the baby of four children!

I would rather listen to rap than Rap City.

1. Have each student complete a mini-autobiography card with these questions: (or use your own)

   a. What are your favorite things to do?

   b. What is something interesting about you that no one in this class knows about?

   c. Where have you lived besides here?

   d. What is the most unusual thing you have ever done or seen?

   e. What do people in this room need to know about you?

   f. What kind of music do you like?

   g. What's your favorite TV show?

2. Type up the answers to each question to create a set of information. Do not put student names with the answers.

3. Hand out the sheets of collected data and tell students their first assignment is to match the names of their classmates to the information.

Hint: A separate list of their classmates' names will help with correct spelling.

This activity can be handed out for homework so that students will talk to each other on the bus, in the hall, and outside of (as well as inside) the classroom. You can add an incentive of some kind for the first five or six finishers if you like.

Strategy #47

Narrative Speech Assignment

Students research a particular aspect of a unit of study, invent a character, and present the research through the character in a first-person monologue. This activity incorporates research, organization, and speaking skills and can be easily adapted for any subject matter.

What to Use

- research materials (books, Internet access, and other resources)
- directions and expectations
- craft materials

What to Do

1. Review with students expectations and requirements. See the following page for a suggested outline for evaluation.

2. Students INVENT a fictional character that is somehow related to westward expansion. Ideas include:
   - a friend or relative of a famous person
   - a traveler on the Oregon Trail
   - a Native American
   - a witness at the Alamo
   - a mountain man
   - a storeowner in Independence, Missouri
   - a relative or friend of someone in your novel

3. Students then add some details to the invented character, including name, age, situation, and important personality traits.

4. Next, students complete RESEARCH! They should add authentic facts, details, and examples to the information in order to make character "come alive!"

5. Students make visual aids to accompany their speech. These may include maps, pictures, crafts, models, or slideshows.

6. Now students are ready to become this character and tell their story to the class in the form of a first-person narrative speech.

Note: This example addresses Westward Expansion. The activity is easily adapted to any specific unit of study.

Evaluating the Narrative Research Assignment

Preparation

_____ Use and documentation of at least TWO sources (including a "Works Cited" page due on speech day)

_____ Appropriate and constructive use of library and computer lab time

_____ In-class notes on one video and one article

Content

_____ Introduction

_____ Who are you?_____

Body

_____ What historical people or events have you seen?

_____ What is it like to be in your situation?

_____ What are the good and the bad things about being you?

_____ Remember to include facts, details, and examples that make you seem realistic.

> **Note:** *Be consistent in your organization. If you are talking about "a day in the life . . ." then stick to that. If you want to talk about your whole life, divide it up logically.*

Conclusion

_____ Sum up your character's situation, philosophy, or future plans

Delivery

_____ Proper length of 3 – 5 minutes

_____ Outstanding poise, eye contact, volume, and rate

_____ An appropriate and interesting visual aid

_____ Enthusiasm!

The Nuts & Bolts of Active Learning
©Incentive Publications, Inc., Nashville, TN

Noun Collages

Students make a collage of NOUNS. It reinforces the scope and variety of nouns while involving students in a hands-on activity.

What to Use

- construction paper • glue • scissors
- old magazines for cutting

What to Do

1. Have students locate and cut out words to include:
   - Five common nouns
   - Five proper nouns
   - Five singular nouns
   - Five plural nouns
   - Five compound nouns
   - Five collective nouns
   - Five possessive nouns

   *All nouns will fit into more than one category. Students will need to choose where they wish to place each one.

2. Students glue the words on the construction paper so that each category is together and somehow separated from the other words. They may draw lines, use pictures, cut out decorations, or devise some other organizational pattern. Each section should be labeled correctly.

3. When students have words in place, they may use pictures of people, places, or things to fill any empty spaces.

Student Tips for Success:

· Use your English text to help you. This activity will be much easier if you are well acquainted with the types of nouns before you begin!

· Cut out words that are easy to read from a distance (at least one-half-inch high or so).

· Spread your collage out so that most of the paper is filled.

Check off words as you find them so that you don't have to continually go back and count!

Order, Please!

Wearing paper plate labels, students literally get themselves in order to show sequence, importance, size, or other concepts of order.

What to Use

- plain paper plates
- hole punch
- heavy string
- thick marking pens

What to Do

1. Prepare paper plates as signs to hang around necks. Punch two holes in each plate and tie string through the holes to make a "necklace."

2. Identify ideas, terms, events, factors, or other components of a process or concept for students to review or demonstrate.

3. Write each of these components on a paper plate.

4. Give plates to a group of students.

5. Give the appropriate instruction for students to get in order. This might be in alphabetical order, in the order of an accurate math sentence, in sequential order, in order of importance, in order of difficulty, or in order of size.

6. At an arranged signal, students in the group examine the components and arrange themselves in order.

7. The rest of the class reviews the result and discusses the accuracy of the arrangement. Members in the arrangement can defend their choices.

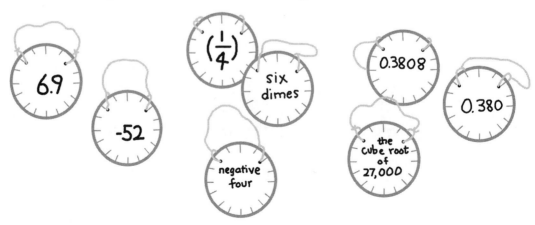

Strategy #50

Parking Lot Math

Students create a huge coordinate grid in the school parking lot and use the grid to show graphing techniques.

What to Use

- a few rolls of duct tape
- several lengths of rope
- several large, colored circles (Frisbees or laminated construction paper circles)
- sidewalk chalk
- wide, open space

What to Do

1. Mark off a giant grid on the parking lot using duct tape.

2. Divide the class into teams of four or five.

3. Give each team a graphing assignment to demonstrate on the human-sized coordinate plane. Each member of a team will represent one of the points of the graph and will present and explain its graph to the other teams. Any type or level of graphing can be demonstrated on the parking lot graph. Students can actually walk to the various areas of the graph and use the large dots to mark points on the graph. They can demonstrate lines or curves by "connecting the dots" with ropes. They can also label points as needed with the sidewalk chalk.

Social studies teachers may want to create a map with lines of latitude and longitude, and have students move to different places on the map.

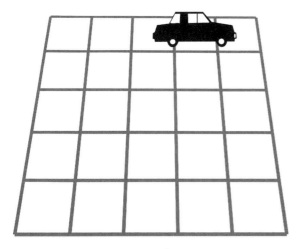

Partner Pairs

Partner pairs is a cooperative and competitive activity in which students work together with partners and teammates to resolve problems, answer questions, or complete tasks assigned by the teacher.

What to Use

- a predetermined list of questions, tasks, or problems for each team to answer or complete

What to Do

1. Divide the class into two teams. Within each team are several partner pairs or small groups of students who will work together to resolve a given problem or complete a specified task. There must be an equal number of groups within each team. The size of the groups depends on the task involved. A class with 28 students might have seven pairs within a team OR a class might be organized into three or four teams with fewer pairs or groups established within each team.

2. Identify teams with a number label, and pairs or groups within each team with a letter. For example, a class might be divided into two teams numbered "one" and "two." Within EACH team, label seven partner pairs—"A," "B," "C," "D," "E," "F," and "G." Each team would then have a pair "A," a pair "B," etc., or pair 1A, 2A, 1B, 2B, etc.

3. Pose a problem or task to the class. Students work together within their smaller pairs or groups to develop a solution. When a reasonable amount of time has passed for the completion of the task, call out a letter. The corresponding letter group for each team runs to the board, works the problem as quickly as possible, and returns to their seats.

4. Scoring is always up to the individual teacher. One point can be awarded to each team that completes the task correctly. Alternatively, two points can be awarded to the team that completes the task first and accurately, with an additional point being awarded to each team that posts a correct or plausible response. For management purposes, it helps to disallow points for any group that cannot keep all of its members seated and relatively silent after posting their response.

Reminder: Make certain that all variations of each letter are called at least once within a class period.

Strategy #52

People Bingo

This variation of Find Someone Who ... is a great icebreaker to get students to know one another.

What to Use

- a copy of a bingo card (page 70) Before you reproduce the bingo card, fill in the squares on the card with unusual things that students are to find out about each other that they normally would not know.

  Example blocks:

    Find someone who has a pet and ask them what the pet's name is. Ask why that name was chosen.
    Find someone with a hobby. Learn about it.
    Find someone who knows a good joke. Have them tell you the joke and then you tell them a joke.
    Find someone who has the same size hand as you do. Are your feet also the same size?
    Find someone who has a favorite song and can hum it to you.
    Find someone who has a favorite meal and what makes it so good.
    Find someone who had a favorite teacher and learn what made that teacher so special.
  - a pen or pencil
  - small prizes

What to Do

1. Provide each student with a Bingo card

2. Designate what type of Bingo game is to be played—four corners, diagonal, vertical, horizontal, or whole card

3. Each student is to find someone who fits the description in each block and have the person sign the square.

4. The first person who completes the chosen game is to yell "Bingo."

5. Once students have fun with the activity, have them discuss the following:
   a. What did you learn about each other?
   b. Were there any surprises?
   c. How can knowing each other better help us work together as a class?

B I N G O

Strategy #53

STUFF

Pile of Stuff

Students create a "pile of stuff" and then use the names of the items as they summarize the concepts they have learned.

What to Use

- "stuff" from around the room gathered by students
- keys, comb, night facial cream, ruler — demonstration pile

What to Do

1. Arrange students in groups of four. If the numbers do not work out, extra groups should have three members. Groups of five are too many for this particular activity.

2. Without telling the students the directions for the activity, have them each find four unusual items in the classroom or their backpacks. The items are placed in the group's master pile. Allow four minutes for this gathering phase. At the end of four minutes, each group should be seated together with a pile of 16 items in the middle of their table. Of course, if the group consists of three members, there will be only 12 items on their table.

3. One the groups are seated with their piles (still without understanding the purpose of the activity), they must come to consensus regarding the eight items that they will use for the activity. This decision phase is funny, as they still do not have any idea what they will be doing with the items, but they must agree on the ones they will be using. When the decision is made, all the extra items are placed off to the side, and the eight chosen are placed in the middle of the table.

4. Explain that groups will create a story or statement that pulls together the important points from a unit just completed, using the "stuff" that they just gathered. Be sure to point out to students that the items may be used not in their literal sense, but rather in a figurative sense. (At this point, the students will have a blank look on their faces, so a demonstration is definitely needed.) Show your demonstration pile. Your "story" might go something like this: As our group was combing through the vast amount of information that was taught during our unit on medieval times, we came upon five key ideas that we think are important. First, the knights were an important part of this time as they fought for the ruler and were, for the most part, very loyal.

5. The lights will go on in the students' eyes, and they will be chomping at the bit to create their group "story." Remind students to think about multiple meanings of the names of the objects and to use, all eight items in their story.

6. Give students about 15 minutes to create their masterpieces. One person must be the recorder and write down the story.

7. Once all groups have completed their stories, give the presentation rules and allow groups a few minutes for practice.

Presentation Rules

- When a group is called upon, group members must hold up each item individually and state exactly what the item is, in its literal sense, so that the entire class can see the items. (This is a key to John's front door.)

- The recorder reads the story, and the person with the "stuff" must hold up the item at the appropriate moment in the story. (The key is held up when the line "we came upon five key ideas . . ." is read.)

- Once all stories have been shared, the entire class should celebrate their accomplishment with applause.

Note: These stories are great to share at an evening curriculum fair. Students love to share them and parents love to hear them! Make certain that all of the "stuff" is available for the evening presentation.

Strategy #54

Pipe Cleaner Sculptures

Students create three-dimensional pipe cleaner sculptures to show their knowledge of a particular topic.

Demonstrate mastery

balance   stability   drag   bow out

air lift   aerodyne   relative wind

heavier-than-air devices

Newton's law of action & reaction

KITE

What to Use

- five to ten pipe cleaners of assorted colors per student (You may wish to buy packs of the long, fuzzy "chenille stems" and cut them in half.)

What to Do

1. Tell the students that they are going to create a 3-D sculpture representing three important points they learned during the unit just completed. Show all of the colors of pipe cleaners that they will be choosing and explain the limit of ten cleaners for their sculpture.

2 The students should draw their ideas for their sculptures and make a list of the colors with quantities that they will be using. They should be given ten minutes to draw their designs.

3. After the planning time, identify groups of students to gather their pipe cleaners from a central location and begin creating. It is faster if pipe cleaners are laid out in piles of like colors and students are brought up to the central location in groups of about five students.

4. The creation phase of this project should be limited to 15 minutes. If, while in the creation stage, a student absolutely needs to use a few more pipe cleaners than the ten allowed, the student must present their dilemma and plead their case for additional pipe cleaners. (You may choose to allow up to a maximum of five more.)

5. Once the sculptures are completed, the student must WRITE an explanation paragraph stating why they chose the three important points and why they created this particular sculpture to illustrate these points. This written assignment will eventually be turned in to the teacher. The students should be given ten minutes to complete the writing assignment.

6. Finally, students share their masterpieces with the entire class and explain their rationale for the sculptures.

7. After all sculptures have been shared, challenge the class to come up with a creative way to display them in the classroom. (They may be hung as mobiles from the ceiling, they may be stapled to colored paper and displayed on a bulletin board, or they may be displayed on a large table.)

A Preposition Is Like a Rattlesnake

Students finish metaphors to make what might seem like far-fetched comparisons. In doing so, they stretch their brains and show the depth of their understanding of learned ideas.

What to Use

Hissss

- a list of key ideas that you want students to review or extend from a lesson or unit
- index cards or half-sheets of paper
- pencils

What to Do

1. Prepare a list of metaphors that require students to make unexpected (and unusual) comparisons of key ideas from a lesson.
2. Write each one of these on a card or half-sheet of paper.
3. Group students in pairs. Give a metaphor to each pair.
4. Direct the pairs to ponder the metaphor and discuss the reason why it is true. Once they agree on the reason, they should finish the metaphor sentences on the paper.
5. Share the metaphors and the student explanations.
6. Take time to discuss the metaphors.

A preposition is like a rattlesnake because . . .

The Declaration of Independence was like a vacuum cleaner because . . .

A crime scene is like an ecosystem because . . .

You could compare a poet to a trapeze artist because . . .

Quadratic equations are less surprising than birthday presents because . . .

A magnet is much like a romance because . . .

A verb is like a headache because . . .

Response Cards

Students work in small groups and respond to questions with numbered cards or by writing numbers on a whiteboard.

What to Use

- a set of five 8 ½ x 11" tag board cards numbered 1 to 5 (the large, easily-to-read numbers should be on both sides of the cards)

OR

- one small whiteboard and one large, dark-colored erasable marker

What to Do

1. Before beginning this activity, develop a number of multiple-choice questions from a unit of study. The multiple-choice answers for each question should be placed on an overhead transparency, on pieces of poster board, on a flip chart, or written on a large white board; a number should be placed by each possible answer, 1-5.

2. Divide class into groups of three or four.

3. Give each group a set of "response cards" or a whiteboard and marker.

4. Ask the first question and reveal the five possible multiple-choice answers. The groups then have 30 seconds to discuss and decide which answer is correct.

5. At the end of the 30 seconds, give a signal, and one person from each group must hold up their card or board that matches the number of the answer chosen by their group. It is EXTREMELY important that ALL cards or boards go up at the same time!

6. You can immediately assess the learning that has or has not taken place and adjust instruction as needed.

7. Reveal the correct answer by holding up the correct number. If a majority of the groups show the correct answer, celebrate their learning. If a majority of the groups show the incorrect answer, verbally take the blame for not teaching the concept well.

> **PLEASE NOTE:** This activity should NOT be used as a contest, pitting group against group. It should be used as a review of learning and a formative assessment strategy. The activity may also be done with individuals rather than groups.

Strategy #57

Save the Last Word for Me

Students work in small groups to actively respond to a reading assignment.

What to Use

- reading text

What to Do

1. Students read a passage, making notations as they go. They identify three or more sentences to which they have a response.

2. Organize students in groups of three to five students. Ask one member of each group to read one line that he or she has identified. The student reads only; there is no commentary or reason for choosing the line given.

3. Each group member other than the reading person responds to that one line—agreeing, refuting, supporting, clarifying, commenting, or questioning.

4. After everyone else has had a chance to make a personal response to the statement, the originator of the line gets to offer his or her commentary—"getting the last word" on the topic.

5. When this round of discussion is done, the next person in the circle calls out his or her chosen line from the text, and everyone responds to the line before this second person offers his or her commentary. Repeat for each member of the group.

Strategy #58

School Staff Interviews

In this interactive-partner or small-group activity, students interview school staff members and share what they learned with the class.

Faculty
Administrators
Assistants
Cafeteria staff
Maintenance
Health Room
Volunteers

What to Use

- interview worksheet (For the best result, develop your own with your students.
- paper and pencil
- clipboards or notebooks

What to Do

1. As a total class, make a list of the different job categories represented by your school staff.

   Faculty (groups can be subdivided by subject matter)
   Administrators
   Administrative assistants
   Cafeteria staff
   Maintenance
   Health Room
   Volunteers

2. Divide the students into interview teams.

3. Choose representatives from each job category and prearrange interview times for the students.

4. Each team will interview school staff in at least two categories.

5. Allow time for practice with interview questions, discussion of appropriate interview behavior, and assignment of questions to team members.

6. Students do interviews.

7. Students share information with discussion of tasks, responsibilities, talents, skills, training, and necessity for each job.

8. Teams write thank-you notes to the persons interviewed.

Strategy #59

School Word Search

In this interactive-partner or small-group scavenger hunt, students interact with the school environment to practice identifying parts of speech.

What to Use

- tasks handout
- paper and pencil

(If clipboards are not available, provide a cardboard square for ease of recording.)

What to Do

1. Create a handout with a series of tasks for student teams.
2. Divide your class into pairs or teams.
3. Give teams a time limit for completing their tasks.

> **Variations:** This search can be done within the classroom. The activity can be extended as homework assignments to include trips to and from school, after-school events, or weekend or holiday activities.

Tasks

1. Search for nouns—things that can be seen, heard, touched, or tasted. (No proper nouns are allowed.) List each noun and its location.
2. Search for verbs—actions seen, heard, or felt. List each verb and its location.
3. Write two possible adjectives for each noun listed in task 1.
4. Write two possible adverbs for each verb listed in task 2.
5. Write five sentences using combinations of words used in tasks 3 and 4.

   OR

6. Create three drawings that illustrate combinations of tasks 3 and 4.

Secret Handshake

Students develop and use a unique handshake that is known only to those in your class.

What to Use

- note pad
- pencil

What to Do

1. A few weeks into the school year, introduce students to the idea of a secret class handshake. Tell them that the time has come for a special way to share and communicate the uniqueness of this group and the bond among you.

2. Let students invent the handshake. Begin by brainstorming possible features.

3. As students brainstorm, the teacher or one student can jot down ideas in a notebook.

4. Review the list of ideas and try out different possibilities.

5. Agree on the final version. Give it a name. (This may be the teacher's name to signify the class.) Practice until everyone has it.

6. Agree that the handshake will be known and shared only among class members. No one else may be taught the secret handshake unless ALL members of the class agree. (For example, students might want to share it with a special classroom visitor.)

7. Use the handshake when you greet each other, when you want to take a break from work, or on other occasions that seem appropriate.

Note of caution: If you plan to try this, and you know there is a gang presence in your school, talk to your police liaison or school counselor so you are aware of gang hand gestures.

Shakespeare Baseball

For this activity, the class is divided into two teams for a "baseball game." This example refers to Shakespeare, but the activity can be used in any subject area.

What to Use

- note cards
- a baseball diamond (You can use masking tape on the floor or, for more calm play, draw the diamond on the white board and move magnets as runners when they "advance.")

What to Do

Part 1 — Writing Questions

- Divide students into groups of three to five and distribute 20 blank note cards to each group.
- Explain that each group's job is to write 20 questions and answers related to the Shakespeare unit just completed. These questions will be used for a "baseball" game, so they need to write 5 questions that will be used as "singles," 5 used as "doubles," 5 as "triples," and 5 as "home runs." Singles are the easiest and home runs the hardest.
- Explain that the categories are somewhat nebulous, but it's up to their group to decide which question fits into which category. Also, all the groups' questions will be combined, so they may have to answer their own question in the game or they may not. You may have more guidelines if needed, such as "singles" should be true-or-false questions, "doubles" should be multiple-choice, or you can leave it to their discretion.
- Have the students write one question on each note card. On one side, put the question and the answer on the other side; label it "single," "double," "triple," or "home run," depending on its difficulty.

Part 2 — Preparation

- Look through and sort the cards. Put all singles together, all doubles, and so forth. Discard any repeats.
- Divide the class into two equal teams.
- Prepare the baseball diamond for play. Flip a coin to see who goes first.

Part 3—Playing the Game

Procedures and Rules

1. Each batter chooses the type of question he or she wants. The moderator (usually the teacher) reads the question. If the batter answers correctly, the batter advances to the appropriate base (either physically or by moving a marker on the board).

2. An "out" is made when a player gets a question wrong. After three outs, the other team gets a turn.

3. Play continues through a given number of innings or for a designated time period.

4. Use these rules to help things run smoothly:

   • The moderator has the final say on the correctness of answers

   • All runners advance the same number of bases, so if a person is on second base and a single is answered correctly, the batter and the runner each advance one base

   • Stealing bases is not allowed.

   • The inning is over after three outs OR after all batters have had a turn (the team has "batted around").

You may want to consider adding these additional rules to balance the teams.

First, the same category of question may not be requested more than once in succession (e.g., two students in a row may not both request singles, etc.). This adds to the variety and ensures more questions are asked.

Second, students have the option of asking their team for help with the home run questions. To balance this out though, it costs the team two outs instead of one if they get the answer wrong. This can also encourage developing strategies (so if a team already has two outs, there is no risk in trying for a home run).

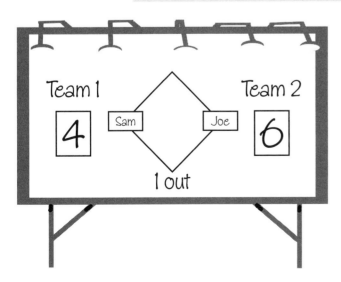

Show Your Power

Students create PowerPoint slides to address and review concepts and objectives.

What to Use

- list of concepts to be addressed
- computers
- LCD projector

What to Do

Note: If students do not have a basic knowledge of PowerPoint, do a basic overview or enlist the help of the technology instructor to give a basic lesson. Be sure that each small group has at least one student familiar with PowerPoint.

1. Divide key concepts equally among the small groups or pairs.
2. Have collaborative groups complete one to two slides per concept that summarize their concept.
3. Put all of the slides together for a class review.
4. Forward the slideshow to the parents and students for at-home review.

Evaluate Level of Understanding

Signs of Progress

Traffic signs help students reflect on the extent of their understanding of concepts or processes.

What to Use

- poster board (white, red, yellow, other colors optional)
- marking pens, crayons, or paint and brushes

What to Do:

1. Get students involved in creating "traffic" signs ahead of time: Prepare these signs: stop, caution, slow, 70 mph, sharp curve, yield.

2. Post the signs on the walls around the room.

3. Prepare a list of topics or questions from a lesson that students should be able to explain or answer.

4. Discuss the use of the signs. Tell students that you will project key ideas, topics, or questions from the lesson, and that they are to stand under the sign that describes their level of understanding. (Agree ahead of time what each sign means.)

5. Project the topics or questions one at a time. Allow a minute for students to reflect on the item.

6. Students move to stand under signs that match their self-reflection.

7. Continue this with other questions.

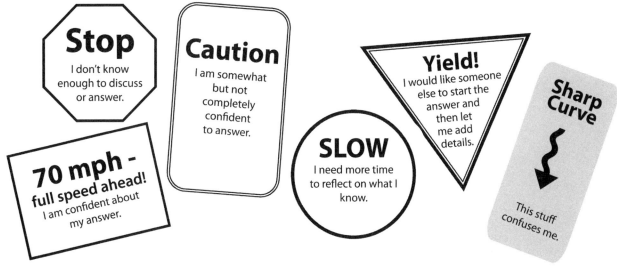

The Nuts & Bolts of Active Learning

Strategy #64

The Single Dot

Students are challenged to use their imaginations and think of as many "right answers" as they can in regard to the meaning of a dot on the board.

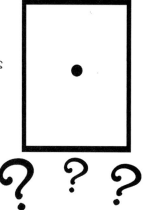

What to Use

- board or a projected slide containing a single dot.
- paper and pencils or pens

What to Do

1. The teacher places a dot on the board or on a slide projected on a screen. It should be in place before the students enter the room.

2. After everyone is settled the teacher asks, "What is that?"

3. Someone will usually reply with an answer like, "It's a dot on the board."

4. The teacher asks if it could be anything else. After the students muse a bit, the teacher announces that this exercise was done with a group of kindergarten students, and they immediately thought of more than 50 things it could be (a bug, the end of a straw, a hatch, a shadow of a round object, part of a musical note, etc.).

5. The teacher asks the students to list as many possible answers as they can within four minutes.

6. After time is called, the teacher asks the students to share some of their responses. Help students appreciate very imaginative responses as well as those that are rather ordinary.

7. The teacher then explains that somewhere between kindergarten and middle school, students seem to lose their ability to look for more than one right answer. Discuss the importance of new and novel thinking as well as the very real possibility that often there is more than one right answer to a problem.

8. Ask students to reflect on their experience by creating a journal entry page, a poem, an essay, a picture, a letter, a song, or any other creative means to communicate their meaning.

For further discussion, read aloud or assign reading from *The Dot* by Peter H. Reynolds. (2003). Boston, MA: Candlewick Press. ISBN 978-0763619619

So What?

A large question mark can be handed to any student at any time during a lesson or discussion. This means that all students must be ready to reflect on the difference that this topic makes in the real world.

What to Use

- large, sturdy pieces of poster board
- scissors
- marking pens
- laminating machine

What to Do

1. Involve students in making some large, sturdy question marks—no less than 18 inches (45 centimeters) tall.
2. Write *So What?* in large letters on both sides of the question marks.
3. Laminate the question marks to make them durable.
4. Discuss what "So What?" means in relation to a new idea, concept, term, process, event, or topic.

FOR EXAMPLE:	What difference does this make?
	What are the implications of this?
	What are the consequences of this?
	What are the possible benefits?
	What is the importance or value of this?
	How will this affect me or others?
	What would happened if this didn't exist?

5. Use the question marks during discussions or reviews. Toss a question mark to a student (or toss out a few at a time). The discussion stops, and the student attempts to give at least one idea in response to the "So What?" question.

Strategy #66

So, Who Has?

This fast-paced, engaging card game can be played in small groups or as a whole class. One student reads or plays his or her card while others listen and watch for a cue to stand and read (or lay down) their cards.

What to Use

- 3 x 5" note cards (20 to 30 depending on how many facts there are)
- marking pen
- 20 to 30 facts

What to Do

1. Create the deck of cards by writing the following on cards:

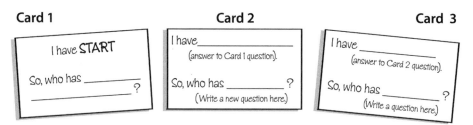

Card 1

I have START

So, who has _____?

Card 2

I have_____ (answer to Card 1 question).

So, who has _____? (Write a new question here.)

Card 3

I have _____ (answer to Card 2 question).

So, who has _____? (Write a question here.)

Continue making cards until you have all facts on cards.

2. Arrange students in groups of four or more (the more players, the easier the game).

3. Shuffle and deal the cards. Depending on the number of cards and the number of players, deal players multiple cards.

4. Players look over cards and then hold them or arrange the cards in front of them.

5. Play begins with the card that says I have START.

6. The student who has that card reads and puts the card down. "I have Start, so who has. . .."

7. The student who has the card with the correct answer, plays it face up on top of the last card and then reads the card aloud, "I have_____, so who has. . .."

8. Play continues until the last card is played.

9. The first person to play all his or her cards, wins the game. (Note: This is completely random.)

10. Shuffle the cards and repeat the game.

Sorting Cards

Students sort facts, concepts, or attributes into categories and defend their reasoning as they designate the appropriate category.

What to Use

- index cards or adhesive notes with individual facts, concepts, and attributes written on them
- category labels

What to Do

1. Teach something that has multiple categories, like types of government, multiple ideologies, cycles in science, systems of the body, taxonomic nomenclature, or multiple theorems in geometry.

2. Display the categories.

3. Distribute index cards. Ask students to work in groups to place each fact, concept, or attribute in its correct category. (The conversation among group members is just as important to the learning experience as the placement of the cards, so let students defend their reasoning orally and often.)

Note: Summarization occurs every time a student lifts an individual card and makes a decision on where to place the card. Students are weighing everything they have been taught as they consider their options. If others question why an individual places a card in a particular category, the discussion furthers the impact.

Example of Topic Categories

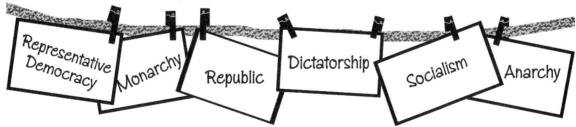

Stand Up and Be Counted

Students formulate an opinion about different topics and take a physical stand. They have the opportunity to see how others in their class have different viewpoints.

Who is better, Batman or Superman?

PC or Mac?

Live without music or live without T.V.?

What to Use

- long line of tape down the middle of the classroom
- set of "either-or" questions (from silly to serious)

What to Do

1. Clear an area in the room and place a long line of tape down the middle of the room.
2. Read a statement with "either-or" answers.
3. Once the statement has been read, students who agree with the first answer move to one side of the taped line, and students who agree with the second answer move to the other side. Undecided students stand on the line.
4. Encourage several students to explain why they chose the answer they did.
5. Repeat with other questions.
6. Complete the activity with a written reflection. Have students reflect on and write the answers to one or more of the following questions:
   - Which question elicited my strongest opinion, and why did I feel so strongly?
   - How did I feel when I was one of the few with a certain opinion?
   - Which question was I undecided about and why?
   - Which question was my favorite and why?
   - Which question response by the class surprised me?

Quickly Demonstrate Level of Understanding or Feeling

Stand Up, Sit Down

This activity gets the kids up and moving and is similar to the "Four Corners" activity but it does not require as much time or preparation.

What to Use

- a set of predetermined questions regarding a particular subject OR a set of controversial statements about a particular topic.

What to Do

1. All students should stand by their desks or tables.

2. Read a question or make a statement to the class.

3. Those students who disagree with the statement, or answer "no" to the question should sit down. Those that remain standing obviously agree with the statement or would have answered "yes" to the question. Begin a brief discussion about the statement OR merely give the correct answer to the question.

4. As with any group activities, adequate wait time is essential. Many students require a moment of reflection before voicing their opinion, especially if it differs significantly from that of their peers.

Stuck On You

Sticky notes serve as the catalyst to help students expand their understanding of material learned and connect it to the real world.

What to Use

- sticky notes containing words or short phrases that name key concepts, ideas, or terms for students to review from a lesson or unit of study

What to Do

1. Put one sticky note on each student desk.
2. When you are ready to start the activity, students stick the notes on their shirts and find a partner.
3. Partners take a moment to examine and read each others' words.
4. Give this direction: look at your partner's word or phrase, and tell something that could CAUSE it.
5. Allow a few minutes for each partner to respond.
6. Give this direction: read your partner's word and tell her or him where you might expect to find that event, idea, or situation occurring.

Variation:

1. Put the sticky notes on students' backs—without their knowing what the notes say.
2. Students pair up with partners.
3. Give this direction: Look at your partner's word and tell a benefit of this.
4. Give this direction: Look at your partner's word and give a consequence for this.

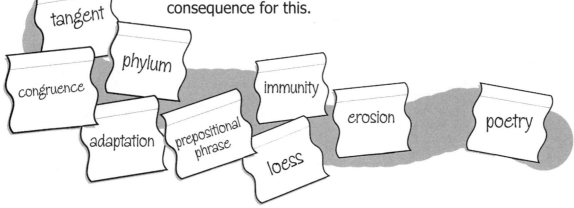

 Strategy #71

Surf's Up!

Students are divided into two teams; they toss a beach ball among themselves until a signal is given, then answer a question determined by the last catch. The friendly rivalry between the two teams heats up as they compete against each other to collect the most points by answering questions correctly.

What to Use

- two inflatable beach balls with colored sections
- marking pen
- sets of questions — 10 to 15 questions for each category
  two red (or a color on the ball) vocabulary questions
  two Blue (or a color on the ball) true/false questions
  two Yellow (or a color on the ball) fill-in-the-blank questions
  two White (or a color on the ball) multiple-choice questions
  two Green (or a color on the ball) previous-chapter questions

  * The categories can be changed to fit your subject area (for example, people or events for history, parts of speech for English, and equation types for math).

What to Do

1. Write the name of one category of question on each section of the inflated beach balls. (For example, red might say *vocabulary*, blue might say *true or false*.)

2. Divide students into two teams. Have each team form a circle.

3. Each team selects a team leader who will take the question sheets and stand outside the circle. That person will read the question, wait for the answer, check the answer, and keep track of the points.

4. Toss one beach ball to each team. The object is to toss the ball among the team, without letting the ball touch the ground.

5. To stop the ball toss, the teacher says, "SURFS UP!" The next student catches the ball and freezes.

6. Call out a finger. (For example, you might say, "right thumb.")

7. Whatever color the student's right thumb is on determines the question type to be answered.

8. The team leader reads the question on the sheet, listens for the person holding the ball to answer, checks the answer, and awards the team one point for a correct answer.

9. The team then starts tossing the ball back and forth again until the teacher says, "Surf's Up!" again.

10. Tally points at the end for a team winner!

Synectics

Students work in small groups to create analogies that require them to think at a high level—to make comparisons between two apparently irrelevant things.

What to Use

- space for groups to meet
- writing paper

What to Do

1. Model the technique.

   Teach a topic to students

   Ask students to describe the topic, focusing on descriptive words and critical attributes.

   Identify an unrelated category to compare to the descriptions students have identified. (Think of a sport that reminds you of these words. Explain why you chose that sport.)

   Students write or express the analogy between the two.

2. Organize students into small groups.

3. As a whole class, brainstorm four objects from a particular category (kitchen appliances, household items, the circus, forests, shopping malls).

4. Have students within the groups brainstorm what part of the information you want them to summarize (a lecture, a reading assignment, a science lab) is similar in some way to the objects listed.

5. Groups each create four analogies, one for each object.

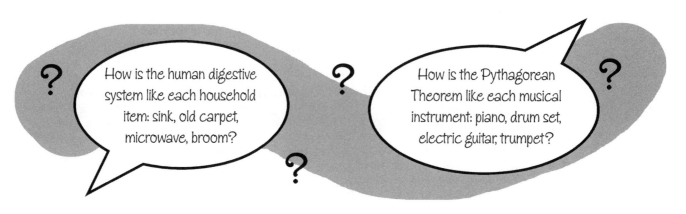

How is the human digestive system like each household item: sink, old carpet, microwave, broom?

How is the Pythagorean Theorem like each musical instrument: piano, drum set, electric guitar, trumpet?

Strategy #73

Take Your Place in Line

Students follow directions to organize themselves without using words.

What to Use

- no materials needed

What to Do

- Teacher gives an oral direction and students are to line up from the door in a particular order, using no verbal communication to find their correct placement in line. Hand gestures are allowed.

- Line up in chronological order by birthday. Begin with January 1 at the door and December 31 farthest from the door. If two or more students have a birthday on any given day, they stand side by side.

Hmmm.
Stripes? Or solids?

- Line up in alphabetical order by the last letter of your last name. Same-letter students organize themselves by the next-to-last letter.

- Count the number of total letters in your name. Line up with least number of letters closest to the door. Same numbers stand side by side.

- Line up by the number of your street address. The largest number should stand closest to the door.

- Line up according to your phone number. The lowest number is closest to the door.

- Group yourselves according to shirt color. Solid colors should be grouped together, stripes together, plaids together, floral prints together, and geometric designs together. Then within your group, get into line in order of the number of letters in the name of the street where you live.

Strategy #74

Talk Show Time!

Students take the role of different characters in a story and pretend that they are guests on a talk show. They answer questions and discuss topics presented by the moderator. The activity can be done in small groups, but is also very effective as an all-class exercise.

What to Use

- no materials needed (unless you want to make a "microphone" prop for the host)

What to Do

1. Arrange the classroom like a stage, with chairs in the front facing the audience.

2. After reading a piece of literature (poem, short story, novel), choose students to play the parts of characters in the piece. This can be done randomly or by using volunteers (the more enthusiastic the participants, the better).

3. Tell the characters that they will be guests on a talk show.

4. Give the characters time to prepare a few notes about "themselves."

5. Give the audience time to write questions for the characters.

6. Choose a moderator or host for the show. (The teacher can start if needed.)

7. Begin the show as a regular talk show would. Have the host introduce himself or herself, and then introduce each person on the "panel."

8. Proceed as a talk show would, with each character talking for a short amount of time followed by audience questions. For variety, you can add "specialists"; for example, if your characters are a dysfunctional family, you could have a "therapist" on the panel giving them advice.

9. For further variety, characters can change every few minutes or audience members can rotate with the panelists.

> **Hints:** In addition to being a fun activity, this is also an excellent way to assess how well students have read something and how well they understand the characters. In a story with less well-developed characters, the students will need to make more inferences about how their character would act, speak, etc.

 Strategy #75

Tell Me More

Success in the classroom starts with relationships. Students choose items from a tub and then give responses associated with the items they have chosen. This is a fun way to get students sharing and learning things about each in other to create an environment that encourages acceptance.

What to Use

- ten different containers of inexpensive items (enough for everyone): pebbles, mini marshmallows, pennies, beans, seeds, paper clips, safety pins, pieces of cloth, little plastic animals, refrigerator letters, little plastic flowers, tickets
- chart that lists the topic associated with each item

What to Do

1. Everyone chooses five items and then takes a seat.
2. Bring out the chart that lists the topic associated with each item.
   pebble = something that happened to you over the summer
   marshmallow = a fun memory from last year
   ticket = your favorite subject in school
   paper clip = the person you tell everything to
   animal = the thing you like to do with your spare time
   cloth = where you would live if you could live anywhere in the world
   seed = what you want to do with your life
   pennies = the person you value most in the world
   letter = a word that starts with that letter that makes you happy
   bean = what you would wish for if you had only one wish
   safety pin = your pet peeve
   flower = one thing about you that we would never guess
3. Students list the five items they have and a response to the corresponding topics.
4. For sharing you might have
   Students find a person they are sitting by.
   Students find a person across the room.
   Students find a person wearing the same color they are.
   Students find a person of the opposite sex.
   Students find a person they have never met.
5. Students write their names on their paper, add anything else they want you to know about them in the extra space, and then turn in the paper.
6. Read the papers to get to know the students in the class.

Option: This activity can also be done using colored beads or colored candies instead of the random items.

Strategy # 76

Thanks for the "Kisses"

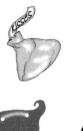

In this brief activity, students show their thanks for each other and recognize how important each person is to effective teamwork.

What to Use

- a bag of Hershey Kisses
- a container for the candy

What to Do

1. Fill the container with Hershey Kisses.
2. Give every student three kisses from the container.
3. Tell students that they are to give each kiss to three other students who have been helpful to them—who have helped them in any way to feel good about this class or school, or have helped them to learn. They may choose to recognize students for any reason.
4. Once students have had some fun giving out their kisses, ask them to stop and discuss the following questions:

   a. How did it feel to get a kiss from someone?

   b. How did it feel to give a kiss?

   c. Were there any surprises for you?

   d. As a person, what can you do to show your appreciation for other students?

   e. As a class, what can we do to show how much we appreciate each other?

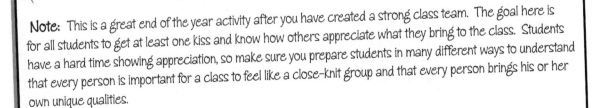

Note: This is a great end of the year activity after you have created a strong class team. The goal here is for all students to get at least one kiss and know how others appreciate what they bring to the class. Students have a hard time showing appreciation, so make sure you prepare students in many different ways to understand that every person is important for a class to feel like a close-knit group and that every person brings his or her own unique qualities.

Tie My Shoe

Tie a shoe? It may seem simple; but in this game, two must work together to tie a shoe faster than the other teams.

What to Use

- several pairs of tennis shoes with laces
- chairs for all students
- clock or timer

What to Do

1. Set chairs up in groups of three chairs in a row.
2. Form teams of three students each.
3. Have students sit in the chairs.
4. The student in the center puts a shoe on one foot. The shoe must remain untied.
5. On a signal to start, the two outside students use their outside hand (the hand farthest from the shoe) to tie the shoe on the foot of the person in the center. ONLY the outside hand is to be used.
6. The team that successfully ties the shoe first is the winner.
7. Try this again, with students switching places among their team's seats.
8. Discuss the process by asking these questions:
   - What made this activity difficult?
   - What was the purpose of the activity?
   - What strategies did you use to be successful?
   - How can you apply such strategies to academics?

Variation: Turn this into a tournament. Rather than have all the students compete at once, let teams try the task in "heats"—perhaps two teams at a time. Then have a "run-off" of winners from each heat. Use the timer to record the time for each successful shoe-tying.

Trigger Letters

Students role-play a situation to activate prior knowledge and relevant background experiences before reading or studying a new topic.

What to Use

- copies of a letter you have created with reference to the content of an upcoming reading selection

What to Do

1. Hand out a letter to students. Have them read the letter and imagine how they would react if they found it on the floor.

2. Pair up students and have them figure out to whom the letter was written and who wrote it, why it was on the floor, what issue is refered to, what they should do with the letter, and what the writer might suggest they do with the letter.

3. Have pairs report on their discussions.

4. Ask, "Who would be interested in this issue?" Generate a list of individuals with a vested interest in the problem.

5. Have individual students choose someone on the list and write about the problem from the viewpoint of the person chosen.

6. After ten minutes, have volunteers share an excerpt from their writing. These readings result in a choral montage of different perspectives on the issue raised.

7. Move on to reading the selection.

Analyzing the letter not only helps students make inferences, it also motivates them to read.

Strategy #79

Twitter It!

When you twitter, you must keep the message succinct. Students practice that skill by summarizing main ideas as if they were about to communicate them through twittering.

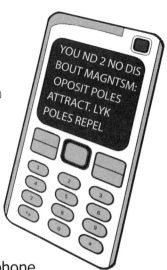

What to Use

- drawings of cell phones
- pencils

What to Do

1. Create and reproduce a drawing of a cell phone.
2. Review the process of twittering with students: A message is prepared to type or text into a computer or cell phone. The message is limited to 140 characters. Text language is allowed.
3. Ask students to prepare a "tweet" that summarizes the main idea of something they have heard, read, or otherwise learned.
4. Students write their messages onto the cell phone drawing—just as they would type them in for sending.

Note: Condensed spellings, symbols, other shortcuts, and the language of texting are acceptable, since the text messages must be kept as short as possible.

Strategy # 80

Turned On, Tuned In

At the beginning of a new topic of study, groups of students list facts or concepts they know about the upcoming topic. During the opening lecture on the topic, students listen for facts and concepts they listed. When the teacher addresses an item on a group's list, group members raise their hands and receive points for their team.

What to Use

- paper for recording group ideas
- markers or pens

What to Do

1. Introduce the topic title and explain that before the class begins studying the topic, you would like to see how much they already know about the topic.

2. Divide students into groups of equal size.

3. Instruct groups to take seven to ten minutes to pool their knowledge and list all the facts they know about the topic.

4. Explain that groups will earn group points toward group grades based on their list of facts.

5. As groups develop their lists, circulate and observe the progress. Announce when groups have only one minute left.

6. Call time. Tell groups to raise hands during the lecture when the lecture covers a point on the group's fact list. Assign a scorekeeper.

7. Deliver the lecture, stopping when group members raise their hands. Allow groups to report what their group said about the fact they listed that corresponds with your lecture point.

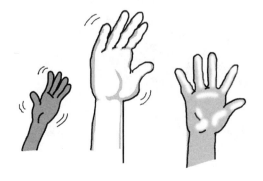

Unforgettable Tunes

Music boosts the memory. Students write their own lyrics for popular tunes to help them remember such things as vocabulary word meanings, math concepts, grammar rules, science concepts, historical facts or sequences, or problem-solving processes.

What to Use

- titles of simple songs, each written on a small index card
- vocabulary terms or key concepts, each written at the top of a large index card
- a basket (or box)
- pens or pencils

What to Do

1. Place the small cards in a basket.
2. Divide students into small groups. Give each group a large index card with a term, concept, or key idea.
3. Each group draws a song title card from the basket.
4. The group works together to write song lyrics to the tune they have chosen. (They write the final product on the large index card.) The song must use, review, or teach the word or concept.
5. Allow plenty of time for groups to sing and share their songs.

VOCUBULARY TERM:
paradox

SONG TITLE:
Jingle Bells

All right, team, let's rap it!

Up in Arms

Students must use ingenuity, communication skills, and cooperation to untangle a mess of arms.

What to Use

- clock or timer

What to Do

1. Students stand and form a tight circle.
2. Ask them all to raise their left hand in the air.
3. Instruct them to point their right hand toward the center of the circle.
4. When all have followed these instructions, tell them to lower their LEFT hand and grab someone else's RIGHT hand.
5. Once this contact is made, they are not allowed to break it.
6. Ask them to hold still and listen. Tell them that, on a signal, they are to untangle themselves without breaking their grip.
7. Start the timer and give the signal.
8. When untangled, the results should be that they are still in a circle, though some members may be facing away from the circle.
9. Try this again and see if they can beat their first time.

Variation: Split the group in half for their first try at this task. It will be easier with fewer people.

Strategy #83

Value Cards

Students trade value cards to create a set of three cards representing the values they most want to possess.

What to Use

- copies of value cards (You will need three cards per student.)

What to Do

1. Discuss with your class how we make many trade-offs in life. We may pursue one value and, as a result, not have time to pursue other values. We may place a priority on one talent and fail to think about how it affects the rest of our lives.

2. Give each student three value cards.

3. Have students walk around the classroom and make trades to accumulate the cards with those values they consider most important.

4. After about ten minutes of trading, call the students back together.

5. Have students write about one trade they would never have made if it had been real life and one trade that they actually would have made.

Note: This is a terrific way to introduce literature about trade-offs— *"The Devil and Tom Walker," The Giver, The Great Gilly Hopkins.*

honesty	bravery	innocence
beauty	humility	health
intelligence	respect	wealth
trustworthiness	friendship	competence
love	family	political power
fame	artistic talents	athleticism

Strategy #84

What I Like About You . . .

Students trade papers and respond anonymously with written positive affirmations to other classmates.

What to Use

- sheets of paper

What to Do

1. Begin with a discussion of appropriate and inappropriate compliments. Include issues of personal privacy, sexism, racism, "back-handed" compliments, and sarcasm.

2. Role-play appropriate ways to receive compliments. Explain that many people have great difficulty receiving positive affirmations from others.

3. Tell the students that they are going to get the chance to receive affirmations in a very nonthreatening method.

4. Ask each student to put his or her name at the top of a sheet of paper.

5. Be sure to participate with the class on this activity. Put your sheet in there, too.

6. At the end of the activity, collect all papers.

7. Ask students to express how it felt to write positive affirmations to others. Why was it easier to write to some than to others? (Speak only in a general sense; do not name anyone specifically.)

8. Pass the papers back to their owners and allow students to read what was written by their classmates. Either out loud or as a journal prompt, allow students to react to what was said to them.

Collect all the papers and give these directions:

- "I am going to pass out the papers randomly. When you receive someone's paper, think about that person and write something affirming to him or her. You must start your statement with the words 'I' or 'You.' You cannot use the words 'he' or 'she.'"

- "When you finish with your message to the person listed at the top of the page, trade papers with someone. Make sure that you never give a paper to the person whose name is at the top. Trade with someone else if you need to."

- "When you trade a paper, read the other statement(s) written previously. Let me know if you have a question about the appropriateness of something written on the sheet. We want to make sure this is a positive experience for everyone involved."

- "Please write something different from the other responses on the page. You can affirm the same attribute, but you must phrase it in a different way or give a different example."

Strategy #85

Without Sense

Students are asked to complete a common task without the help of a normally used sense.

What to Use

- no materials needed

What to Do

The teacher asks the students to attain a group goal without the use of a particular sense.

Examples:

1. Students are asked to form a chronological birthday line without any talking.
2. Students either blindfold themselves or close their eyes and form a line from tallest to least tall (without looking).
3. Students are asked to group themselves according to shoe size without any talking.
4. Students either blindfold themselves or close their eyes and form a perfect square.
5. Students are asked to play the game of "Knots" (getting in groups of eight, clasping hands, then untangling themselves without breaking hands) without any verbal communication.

Students then debrief about what it felt like to operate as a group without the help of a commonly used sense. Questions they may discuss are:

1. What did it feel like to have to communicate in a way different from what you normally do?

2. Who were the best communicators in the group? Why?

3. Who took on the leadership roles in the group? Why did others follow them?

4. Was there anything you wanted to tell the group that you couldn't?

5. Are words the only way we have of "talking" to each other? Explain.

6. When you can't "see," do you listen better? Why?

Word Part Hop

Students "play" a paper-and-pencil partner game to practice identification of parts of speech of words as they are used in sentences.

What to Use

- game-board worksheet for each set of players (page 107)
- pencils
- small playing piece for each player (peas, candy dots, M & M's)
- index cards or strips of paper for sentences
- point assignments posted in room

What to Do

Preparation

1. Reproduce the game-board worksheet
2. Write the sample sentences on index cards or strips of paper.
3. Assign partners for game "play."

The Game

- The players each choose a sentence card and take turns moving their markers along the game board according to the parts of speech represented by the words in the sentence. For example, the first player takes the first word and places his or her marker on the first space on the game board that indicates the word's part of speech; the second player does the same with his or her sentence. (This move may be before or after the first player's marker.) The game continues with players taking turns reading the next word and placing new markers on the word part names as they move toward the finish.

- As one sentence is completed, another sentence card is chosen.

- The game continues until a player reaches the final circle.

- Players count the number of each part-of-speech space covered with their markers and then tabulate their scores using the point chart.

  The game can be "quick" practice or an extended practice activity, depending on the number of sentences, parts of speech assigned to the game, or point values assigned to the parts of speech. All skill level abilities can be addressed with the same game through careful partnering and sentence choices assigned.

The young man quietly sang sad love songs to a happy audience.

The talented artist carefully painted the beautiful sunset.

Sue and Mary happily played a complicated game on the computer.

Joe, Tom, and Sally went to see a very scary movie at the theater downtown.

The ball went high in the air and landed with a thump in the backyard.

The little boy was very sad because he had lost his black and white spotted puppy dog.

Jean and Joan ate two orders of fish and chips with gusto and then drank sixteen glasses of dirty water.

At midnight, the clock in the tower on the church struck twelve times.

William and Henry had red hair and blue eyes, but their younger sister, Sarah Jean, had brown hair and green eyes.

Tony loudly reported that the next-door-neighbor's big, bad dog ate his math homework fourteen days in a row, but the wise old teacher had her doubts!

Points Earned:

Noun	= 1
Verb	= 2
Adjective	= 3
Article	= 4
Adverb	= 5
Preposition	= 4
Pronoun	= 2
Conjunction	= 3
Interjection	= 6

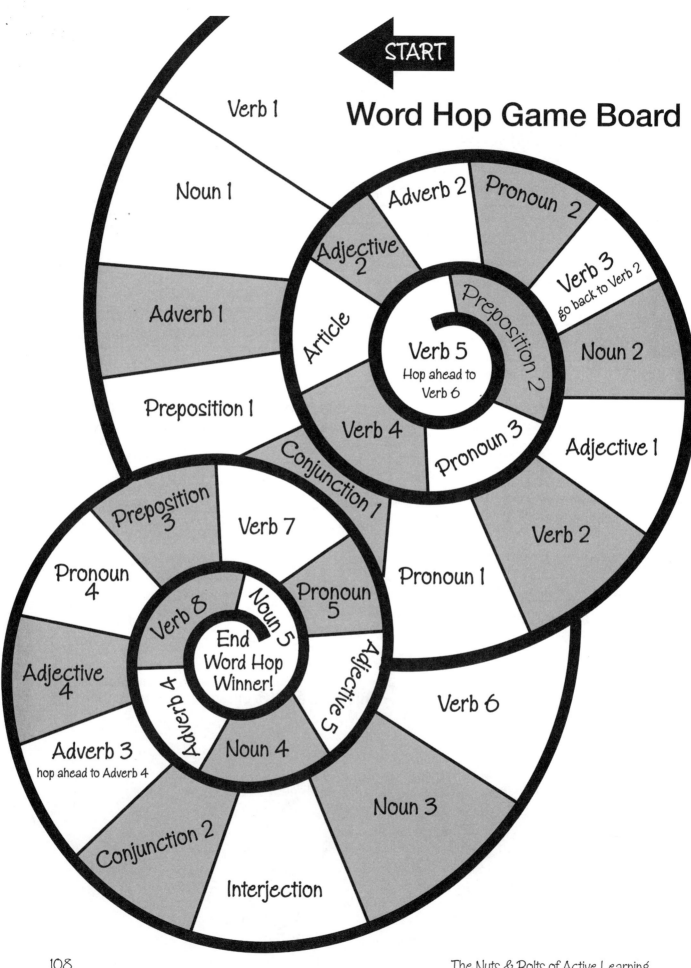

START

Word Hop Game Board

Verb 1

Noun 1

Adverb 1

Preposition 1

Adjective 2

Adverb 2

Pronoun 2

Verb 3
go back to Verb 2

Article

Verb 5
Hop ahead to Verb 6

Preposition 2

Noun 2

Verb 4

Pronoun 3

Adjective 1

Conjunction 1

Pronoun 1

Verb 2

Preposition 3

Verb 7

Pronoun 5

Pronoun 4

Verb 8

Noun 5

End
Word Hop
Winner!

Adjective 5

Adjective 4

Adverb 4

Verb 6

Adverb 3
hop ahead to Adverb 4

Noun 4

Noun 3

Conjunction 2

Interjection

Strategy #87

Xs and Os

In this game show format, students become a giant tic-tac-toe board and play the game with an academic twist!

What to Use

- four sets of nine questions with the correct answers
- nine large X cards
- nine large O cards

What to Do

1. Select nine students who will become the nine squares in the tic-tac-toe board. Arrange their desks in the typical tic-tac-toe grid. Each of the nine students should have an X and an O card.

2. Explain to the tic-tac-toe square students that they will be called on and a question will be read. They may choose to answer the question correctly or bluff an answer. In order to make it more difficult for the teams to decide if they are telling the truth or not, encourage students either to act confident, giving reasoning behind their answers, or to act unsure.

3. Select one student to be the game show host. This student will have all the questions and answers; she or he will read them and moderate the game.

4. Divide the other students into two teams.

5. Select one team to go first.

6. The first team selects a square to answer its first question.

7. The host asks the question, and the square selected gives an answer (real or bluff).

8. The team decides if the square is telling the truth or bluffing. (They agree or disagree with the square.)

9. The host reads the correct answer. If the team is correct, they earn the square, and it is the next team's turn. If the team is not correct, the other team earns the square and gets the next turn.

10. Teams continue to play until a team has three in a row or the board is full. If there is no tic-tac-toe winner, the team with the most squares earns the win.

11. Once that game is done, rotate students to a different position and begin with the second set of questions.

Variation: If the team thinks an answer is being bluffed, they must correctly answer the question to earn the square.

Do You Speak Nuts and Bolts?

An arrangement of nuts and bolts is the centerpiece for a challenging activity that demands good communication and problem-solving skills.

What to Use

- a collection of large nuts and bolts, divided into two bags
- a table with two chairs on each side
- stand-up cardboard divider

What to Do

1. Set up the table with a divider in the middle. It is important that the divider be at head level, so students sitting on one side of the divider do not see students on the other side.

2. Send two students to sit behind the divider. Give them a few minutes to build an arrangement of nuts and bolts.

3. Seat two other students opposite the divider. It is important that they do not see the arrangement. Give this pair the other bag of nuts and bolts.

4. The task of the students who see the arrangement is to communicate to the other pair how to build an identical arrangement. The task of the other group is to listen and follow directions. (Other class members observe one side or the other.)

5. Allow a reasonable amount of time for the task. Remove the divider. Involve the whole class in a discussion of the process and the results.

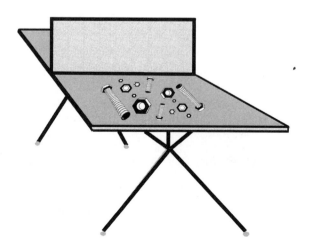